ORTUS

First published by Ortus 2025

Copyright © 2025 by Leilah van der Schyff

All rights reserved. No part of this publication may be reproduced, stored or transmitted in any form or by any means, electronic, mechanical, photocopying, recording, scanning, or otherwise without written permission from the publisher. It is illegal to copy this book, post it to a website, or distribute it by any other means without permission.

Leilah van der Schyff asserts the moral right to be identified as the author of this work.

Leilah van der Schyff has no responsibility for the persistence or accuracy of URLs for external or third-party Internet Websites referred to in this publication and does not guarantee that any content on such Websites is, or will remain, accurate or appropriate.

Designations used by companies to distinguish their products are often claimed as trademarks. All brand names and product names used in this book and on its cover are trade names, service marks, trademarks and registered trademarks of their respective owners. The publishers and the book are not associated with any product or vendor mentioned in this book. None of the companies referenced within the book have endorsed the book.

First edition

Contents

Preface	iii
Prologue	1
Coloured	3
Why are you not dancing?	11
Appeliepies in the garden	17
Milo's daughter	25
The school of logic and magic	34
Then the world turned digital	39
Like I belonged in this wealthy world of college	44
Public transport	52
Why do you keep you White?	57
Class of 2005	61
A Diploma in Journalism	64
Fang, the border collie	69
A girl should know how to drive	73
We were going to make ads	80
Janazah prayers and rejection letters	86
The rise of social media	96
Be sure not to burn out before you are fully lit	103
Becoming best in class	110
I'm in the business of boosting revenue	114
Breaking the glass ceiling	119
Soaring, on a global scale	125
Imposter syndrome enters the chat	131

You don't get what you don't ask for	135
The interview	139
Circus Charlie and visa applications	143
This is a Piccadilly line service to...Cockfosters	150
A matchbox in Notting Hill	162
You'll never see it all	170
Where are your creative values?	178
You won't fit in with the culture	185
Nothing is guaranteed, not even tomorrow	197
A new job and Obsessive Compulsive Disorder	201
The pandemic	208
Each one help one	217
The long pause	223
Overthinking in technicolour	229
Take only what you need	235
All we have is now	237
The morning commute, a cup of coffee, the smallest mundane...	245
Two years without a permanent job	251
The truth about being mixed race	255
For girls like me	260
To new beginnings	266
Afterword	270
Acknowledgements	274
About the Author	276

For the wild ones –
who dream loudly, and live unapologetically.

Preface

Apartheid was a system of laws that focused on racial segregation and discrimination, governing South Africa from 1948 to the early 1990s. The word itself means "*apartness*" in Afrikaans, and the system was designed to ensure White political, economic and social dominance. Under apartheid, the population was divided into four racial categories: White, Black, Indian and Coloured. Every South African was assigned one of these identities, which determined where they could live, work, study and whom they could marry.

Key laws included:

- **The Population Registration Act (1950):** Classified all South Africans by race.
- **The Group Areas Act (1950):** Enforced residential segregation, forcing millions of non-White families out of their homes and into townships (under-developed neighbourhoods)
- **Pass Laws:** Required non-White South Africans to carry identification documents at all times to enter White areas, severely restricting movement.
- **The Bantu Education Act (1953):** Created a racially segregated education system, deliberately underfunding schools for Black and Coloured children to limit future

opportunities.
- **Job Reservation:** Certain professions and industries were legally reserved for White workers, while people of colour were pushed into low-wage, unskilled labour.

Daily life under apartheid was tightly controlled, from beaches and buses to hospitals, parks, and even park benches which carried "Whites Only" signs. Resistance was brutally suppressed: activists were imprisoned, banned or killed. Being Coloured meant living in the in-between. We were not White enough to benefit from privilege, not Black enough to belong to the majority. It meant forced removals, families uprooted from homes and relocated to dusty townships on the city's edges. It meant limited schools, limited jobs, limited futures. It meant being told, daily and officially, that you were less.

Apartheid ended formally in the early 1990s after years of internal resistance and international pressure. In 1994, Nelson Mandela became South Africa's first democratically elected president. But while the laws were dismantled, apartheid left a legacy of inequality in housing, education, wealth and opportunity - divisions that remain deeply felt to this day.

For those of us who grew up in its aftermath, the word *Coloured* still lingers; stamped on our identity and woven into our sense of belonging. Today, it lives silently in the geography of South African cities, in the quality of education, in the wealth gap, and in the unspoken hierarchies that continue to shape opportunity.

v

Prologue

The beginning. As I sit in my sun-drenched garden room in the leafy suburb of South West London, with Sutro, my beloved Chow Chow, sprawled contentedly at my feet, the soft notes of acoustic music playing in the background, and the gentle summer breeze rustling the curtains, it's difficult to pinpoint the exact moment it all began. Life had been so seamless, so effortless lately, that complacency had almost set in. Almost.

"What do you feel like eating? Pizza or Raj's?" MJ asks, wandering into the room with his phone in hand.

"Hmm. I was thinking Mexican?" I reply.

"I'll never say no to Mexican food," he grins, tapping his phone to place the order. "How's the book coming along?"

"Nearly there," I say, my fingers poised over my laptop keyboard, ready to continue weaving the tale that has consumed my days and nights.

Looking out the French doors, into the distance in the garden, I recognise my privilege. I don't allow myself to get smug. I'm grateful for everything; a roof over our heads, safety and security and jobs that pay the bills while also fuelling our passions. I'm not oblivious to the luxury of being able to order take-out regularly whilst also having groceries in the cupboards. Moreover, we're healthy, our dog is healthy and our families in South Africa are healthy. Post-pandemic, these are the only things I need. These are all the little things that I pray for every night when all the world would be sleeping. Life's fragility has taught me to cherish these blessings with a fervour I never knew before. This, and slow Saturdays in London, like today. I realise that this is all I need in order to be truly happy.

I always tell people that this was never supposed to be my life. I didn't have the odds stacked in my favour. I wasn't born with privilege or money. My family wasn't rich or anything, but we got by. Maybe, that's the beginning. So that's where I'll start.

Coloured

I grew up in Wynberg, a residential area in Cape Town, South Africa designed for the working class. Wynberg was separated into upper and lower Wynberg — a segregation of wealth and race, and we lived on the wrong side of the railway tracks. On the other side lived the affluent White population in their beautiful mountain-view homes. The segregation was a result of apartheid: an authoritarian system of racial discrimination that governed South Africa, which systematically privileged White citizens while oppressing people of colour. In this system, White South Africans had the highest status, followed by Indian, Coloured and Black South Africans. Coloured was the term the government used to describe people of colour who were not Black, Indian or Asian. I am Coloured.

In the global north, that can be a derogatory term, but where I come from, it's an identity. A unique identity. It's [1]*Aweh!* when

---

[1] South African slang (originating mainly from Cape Town), used as a friendly expression and can mean different things, like "hello," "goodbye," "cool," "thanks," or "cheers," depending on context.

we see each other in the street. It's a masala steak [2]gatsby cut in four to share with the *brasse* (good friends). It's [3]koeksisters and coffee on a Sunday morning. It's Wembley Roadhouse on a Saturday night with our pimped out cars that were so lowered to the ground the car had to crawl over the speed bumps. It's the [4]Kaapse Klopse on Tweede Nuwe Jaar[5]. It's the way we celebrate things. The big sense of community. The flavours, the colours, the language that only makes sense to us. I grew up learning to identify as Coloured. I ticked the boxes next to *Coloured* on the forms where it asked for my race. When there was no option other than White or Black, I ticked Other. I never really knew what Coloured meant until I started school and learnt about the colonisation of South Africa.

When South Africa was under Dutch Colonial rule, before it fell to the British Crown, the Dutch brought people over from countries like Malaysia, Indonesia, Madagascar, Mozambique and India. The Dutch kept my people as their slaves, which started the slave trade in South Africa. The slaves were then dispersed and picked up English and Dutch as their first

---

[2] A foot long sandwich filled with (mostly) anything you want.

[3] A traditional South African sweet treat: twisted or plaited dough, deep-fried until golden and soaked in spiced syrup. In Cape Town's Coloured communities, koeksisters are often shared on Sundays or at family gatherings.

[4] The Cape Minstrel Carnival, a vibrant New Year celebration originating in the 19th century, when enslaved people were given a day off after New Year's to parade through the streets in bright satin uniforms, playing banjos and drums.

[5] A celebration held on the 2nd of January each year to watch the Kaapse Klopse - one of Cape Town's oldest and most significant cultural traditions.

languages, eventually losing their Asian identities over the years. Many of the slave women were left pregnant as a result of interracial relations with Western men. Whether those relations were consensual or not has not been recorded. But we can all guess. In Cape Town, a large percentage of people of colour, or Coloureds, are descendants of the slaves. There are many subgroups of Coloured people in South Africa. I'm part of a subgroup called Cape Malay, which I think means that my ancestors were mostly Malaysian. I don't really know much about my ancestry. Another subgroup descended directly from the first aboriginal tribes of Africa, the Khoisan. But the vast majority of the Coloured race are descendants of slaves and political prisoners. To South Africa's White-led government, we were labelled non-Whites - a term that stripped us of identity and placed us outside the privileges of citizenship.

After English, Afrikaans is the most common language of Coloureds. The origins of Afrikaans is rich and complex, steeped in the history of colonialism and cultural exchange. One compelling theory suggests that the language was forged in the crucible of oppression, born from the need for enslaved peoples to communicate clandestinely amidst the watchful eyes of their oppressors. To circumvent the language barrier imposed by their captors, these resilient souls drew upon the linguistic mosaic of their homelands, blending elements of Dutch with seafarer languages such as Malay, Portuguese, Indonesian, and indigenous African tongues. The resulting amalgamation, known as Afrikaans, became a tool of survival and resistance, a secret code that allowed the oppressed to communicate freely and preserve their cultural heritage in the face of adversity. For a while, Afrikaans was the language spoken by us peasants, until the White man made it theirs. But there are many origin stories for Afrikaans.

Brown is the term they used to call us — die kleurlinge, die bruinders. The brown ones. The Cape Coloured people of South Africa. Brown is not a term that I identify with when I think of my own race. Brown is a complete, whole colour. It's untampered with. Full. Absolute. And being a descendant of slaves, I think I might be made up of at least two or more races. Brown doesn't accurately represent who I am, not the way Coloured does. I later learned that mixed race is a better, or more politically correct, description of who I am and so I started calling myself mixed. But as a child I just went through life feeling like an outsider, not White or Black.

My family ended up in Wynberg the same way all Coloured families did. During apartheid, the government relocated millions of people of colour, forcing them out of the properties that they owned and into strictly segregated neighbourhoods. People of colour were not allowed to live anywhere they wanted to; they could only live with other people of colour in approved neighbourhoods. This policy is known as the Group Areas Act. It authorised the forced removal of people of colour from desirable neighbourhoods, reserving those areas exclusively for White residents. Today, even though apartheid has been banished for years, you'll still see a big divide in race when passing through the neighbourhoods of Cape Town. Apartheid laws were vile and inhumane, and it left people of colour without a voice to speak up against the inequality. People of colour were stripped from their citizenship status, even though they were born in South Africa, so they couldn't vote for a better government.

And this madness continued until the early 90s, when I was a toddler. I don't remember much of apartheid when I was growing up. I sometimes forget that I was born during the regime. I remember going to school and everyone in my class being more or less the same colour as me. I never saw or interacted with anyone of a different race until I was much older. My family were different shades of brown, some were darker in complexion and some were fairer in complexion like me. And that's about as much diversity I was exposed to as a child.

I had a normal upbringing that came with all the normal generational trauma that Coloured people inherit from years of living in a toxic system as second-rate citizens. Wynberg was a decent area from what I can remember. We lived on a quiet street, where we knew all our neighbours and everything that happened in their lives. We played with the neighbours' kids, made mud pies in the summer in my [6]ouma Dia's garden and we'd queue in aunty Nisa's kitchen on Sunday mornings to buy her koeksisters and twisties, a Cape Town-style plaid doughnut deep-fried in oil, then soaked in sugar syrup and covered in desiccated coconut. It's also a common dessert in China, Korea, Vietnam and the Philippines.

Wynberg was one of those neighbourhoods that was distinctly

---

[6] An Afrikaans term meaning "grandmother," - the matriarchal strength that holds families together, the keeper of stories, traditions, and Sunday lunches.

in the middle of the poverty line. There were other Coloured neighbourhoods in the city that were more impoverished, and there certainly were neighbourhoods that were more upscale. People who lived in Wynberg were seen as too poor to be rich, but too rich to be poor. A metaphor for my life, really. Too White to be Black, too Black to be White. And always too this to be that.

As an only child, I was never lonely. We lived in a separate entrance at the back of ouma Dia's house, in the servant's quarters. Many older homes were designed this way; it was not a reflection of our economic status. The main house was just across the courtyard where my ouma Dia, her brother [7]Amie Salie, her sister Aunty Weya, and my mum's younger siblings lived before they got married and moved away. The house was always full. Every Friday afternoon ouma Dia made minced beef curry with powdery, flaky rotis for lunch. I spent a lot of time in the main house. I was the only child in the family for a long time; my parents had me when they were young themselves. And so I grew up mostly with old people, my ouma and Amie Salie and their friends. My grandfather, ouma Dia's husband, my mum's dad, passed away before I was born, and when my mum was only a teenager. Cancer. My mother first encountered the word as a young girl, not through gentle explanation but through her own determined curiosity. She spent an entire day at the library, poring over medical journals and translating complex papers into words she could understand. Only then did she piece together the meaning of

---

[7] A term of respect and affection used in Cape Town's Coloured communities, similar in meaning to "uncle".

what she had overheard — the reason she had found her own mother weeping into the telephone, telling someone that my grandfather had been diagnosed.

When you grow up with old people you develop a kind of mature outlook on life. I was a loner, I enjoyed my own company. I struggled to find things in common with the other children my age. The things they were interested in, like climbing trees and catching insects, grossed me out. I preferred to sit indoors, drawing, reading or building puzzles. I found people my own age inanely boring.

As a child I've always had a way with words. As soon as I learnt how to write, I wrote a lot. When I put pencil to paper, the words flowed effortlessly onto the paper like magic. I thought that this was expected behaviour and that everyone could do this with words. And so I never really recognised writing as my talent. My thing. Writing helped me express feelings that I struggled with internally and when my voice failed me, which was every time. I wrote poems, stories, letters and songs. I wrote to my friends at school, when I eventually learned to appreciate the friendship of people my own age. I wrote to pen pals in other countries whom my mum would set me up with. I wrote on the bathroom walls of public restrooms and carved words into the wood of my primary school desk.

When I graduated primary school, my English teacher pulled me aside and gave me my very first book. My own book, with my name written inside, that I could keep at home for as long as I wanted because it was mine. It wasn't borrowed from the library or the school, it was all mine. It was called The

Oxford Children's Book of Famous People: 384 pages of famous men and women like musicians, artists, philosophers, sports heroes, scientists and more. It was pages and pages of biographies of these famous people's lives and their achievements. And I wondered why my teacher chose this specific book for me, on our graduation day.

On rainy days, I felt the most inspired. It was when I did my best writing. There was something about the mood a grey sky created that pulled the depths of my soul outside my body and onto paper. That's when I wrote the poem that was included in the Children's Book of Poems in South Africa. And that's honestly where I thought my writing would end. That would be it for me, in terms of the world seeing my words. My mum never imagined a career in writing for me and neither did I.

Why are you not dancing?

~ 1999 ~

The school yard buzzed with excitement as the Grade 9s filled in the courtyard. We were told to sit down in our respective class lines on the worn out tarmac. It was a typical summer's day in Cape Town, South Africa. The sky was a perfect blue above my head, signifying the start of summer and the start of the school year. My class, Grade 9C, were seated east of the podium, just below the basketball post which, thankfully, provided some shade from the harsh sun at 10am in the morning. I shuffled around on the tarmac trying to get comfortable. I crossed my legs in front of me, searching for a spot where the loose stones wouldn't dig into my ankles. I pulled my blue and white chequered dress down to cover my knees as I looked up waiting for the assembly to start.

"Good morning, Livingstone High School!" Principal Hendricks announced as she stepped onto the concrete podium. "Welcome back from summer break. I hope you all had a lovely holiday with your families and are feeling refreshed to take on the new year."

Soft, polite laughter erupted from the crowd of teenagers on the tarmac.

"This is a very exciting year for Grade 9s as you get to choose the subjects that you'll take with you to [8]matric. And that will set the foundation for your university studies."

Assuming that everyone sitting on the ground here will go to university, I thought. Fair enough, this is a good school in Claremont, most of the teens that went there were middle class. But not all of us were. I remember my mum had to use one of her wealthier cousin's home addresses as proof of residence when she battled to get me accepted into Livingstone High School. My mum wanted me to go to Livingstone because her father went there. At the time he was the only person of colour at the school. When I went, it was pretty much a school for affluent Coloured people. And me.

I listened to Principal Hendricks talk more about how the subjects you choose now will set you up for success in your tertiary education, and how we should think well about what we wanted to be when we grew up. As a 14 year old, I had no idea what I wanted to be when I grew up. All around me, my fellow classmates discussed which subjects they'd drop and which they'd keep. If they'd do higher grade or standard grade?

I glanced over to where the Grade 9 As and Bs sat. They would be able to keep art until they graduated high school. I wished I

---

[8] The final year of high school (Grade 12) and the completion of the National Senior Certificate.

were in an art class. Art was not on the list of subjects for me when I first enrolled. The subjects my mum chose for me were: English, Afrikaans, German, Maths, Chemistry and Biology. The line up that gets you to university. The line up that gets you a job in medicine, engineering, accounting or the likes. As a last rogue attempt, I was able to sneak in German as a third language. I was taught that art was a privilege and not a subject we focus our efforts on when preparing for the real world outside of high school. Art was something you did in your free time. Art was not going to get you a real job, is what I was always told to believe. I didn't have any exposure to art or design in any format at school for the same reasons. So I started to tell myself that if I didn't have any experience in art, I had no business thinking about art now. Without any experience in art, I probably wouldn't be good at it, I thought. And this is what grounded me throughout school when I'd rather be doing art. The closest thing to a creative class for me were languages: English, Afrikaans and German. I loved creative writing in all the three language classes I took. That's where my talent really came to life. I was able to flex that creative muscle in ways I never knew existed. My language teachers were fond of me. Often, they'd give me extra books after class and I'd look forward to reading them when I got home. I was terrible at maths and science. But I excelled in the art of languages. Those were also the only classes I truly enjoyed.

Throughout my high school years I wondered what life would be like in the art classes. Sometimes I'd have maths crossover with some of the students in the art classes. Mo and I shared a desk and I'd always pay more attention to his random pencil doodles on his worksheet than trying to solve for x on the blackboard ahead of us. I wanted so badly to be able to sketch like that. But when I tried to sketch, the picture almost never turned out the way I imagined it in my head. Art and design was an unrequited love for me. As much as I was warned against it, I loved art and design, but it didn't love me back.

Meanwhile in German class, my teacher translated the entire *Meet The Beatles!* album to German and taught us how to sing it. Singing *komm gib mir deine hand* is still my favourite and only party trick. Languages made me realise that there is so much beauty in words too. So I thought that if I couldn't be creative with visuals, I'd go all in with words.

I don't remember many defining moments from high school. Except that I had a best friend, we wrote each other letters, we had private nicknames for each other, we stayed at each other's houses and we went to the cinema together. That was about as much freedom two teenage girls would get in my culture. We're still friends today.

I was quiet and awkward at school. I wasn't smart enough to be a nerd, but I wasn't outgoing enough to be in the popular crowd. As far as high school stereotypes go, I was probably the misfit. My group of friends didn't fit one specific stereotype either, some were popular, some were more nerdy, and some were just the girl next door, but we fit together for some reason. Outside of school I had a different set of friends who were wildly more popular. Because of them I found myself at a different house party almost every weekend; the kind of parties where there's a smoke machine and a strobe light and a teenage DJ playing trance classics of the 90s. For a socially awkward person, this was the epitome of hell. Though I did appreciate the vocals of Ian Van Dahl's Castles in the Sky, I hated having to answer the question I was asked at all of these parties,

"Why are you not dancing?"

I pretended that I didn't like the song, but really, I didn't know how to dance. I just don't think my body was able to move in that way, with palms finning in front of your face or whatever the latest move was that week, and I wasn't prepared to try any of it. I put myself in these scenarios often, as a quest to fit in. I said yes to the boys who asked me to be their matric ball date, and then I'd sit by myself at the table while I insisted they could go on and dance without me. I was a terrible matric ball date, but I think I looked okay in photos, and I figured this was probably why I got asked. I still felt like a misfit despite trying to fit in throughout high school.

In my final year of high school, I was faced with the same scenario as before in Grade 9. I watched as my fellow classmates filled out their applications for university and colleges. Everyone seemed so sure of where they wanted to go and what they wanted to study.

One day, towards the end of Afrikaans class, my teacher called me to his desk while everyone else continued to work on their assignments.

"You're doing really well in class," he said.

"Thank you, sir." I replied.

"Have you applied to any colleges, universities?" he continued.

"No,, I haven't."

"What does your dad do?"

"He's an architect, sir."

"And your mom?"

"My mom's a saleslady."

"Students have already completed their applications for the University of Cape Town, the University of Western Cape and so forth. There's still time, so think about it."

"Yes, sir."

I walked away from that conversation knowing that I distinctly would not think about my application to university. There was only one place I really wanted to go. And that wasn't university. It was Ad School.

Appeliepies in the garden

~ 2002 ~

It was after 7pm in our family home in Kent Road, Wynberg. We'd just finished supper: red lentil dahl and fresh white bread. My mum made a little more than usual, so that we could have toasted dahl sandwiches the next day. It was always better the next day. I sat on the beige carpet of my small bedroom with my mum as we spoke about my options for studies after I graduated high school. We needed to make plans for after school, so that I could get a good job, earn decent money and live happily ever after. Money is security, and I got the feeling that my mum wanted this for me. She told me to take subjects that would steer me towards a career in sciences or engineering. Those were the highest paying careers in South Africa, and those were the fields that she wanted me to go into. Dependable careers that provided financial security. Creativity was not a recognised talent. There were no dependable careers in creativity, especially not for people of colour. But I needed to take a chance.

"I think I want to study advertising." I said, a boulder rolling off my shoulders.

My mum looked confused. "You need to study civil engineering, like Zahier. He's very successful at Eskom, and he could put in a good word that could help you to get a full bursary with them, so your studies would be paid in full. And when you're done studying, you could even apply for a job at Eskom too. You'd have money, security, you'd be set for life!"

Eskom is South Africa's sole public electricity supplier. They supply the entire nation with electricity and everyone who worked at Eskom was highly sought after. Zahier was a senior engineering director at Eskom and married to my mum's youngest sister. He is very respected in our family, and he represented success for Coloured people in an early post-apartheid world.

"How would I even get in? I'm not any good at science. And I don't enjoy it. And you need that to get into a Civil Engineering program at university." I said, sounding a bit hopeless.

The prospect of being financially secure for the rest of my life, or at least the near future, sounded dreamy. But my heart wasn't into the idea of engineering as a career. I thought about all the joy I experienced in my language classes over the years at school. And of how I struggled to even pass my maths and science exams. I remember conversations with Mrs Fig, my English teacher, about how she studied copywriting before deciding to teach. She told me about her youthful days at the ad agencies she's worked at, the commercials on TV that she helped create, and how much fun she had all those years ago. I thought about how she saw me in a career like that, with my talent for writing.

I knew I wanted to do that. And maybe I didn't know this back then, but my path into advertising would be so different to my White English teacher's path - shaped not by privilege or easy access, but by obstacles I had yet to face. Maybe I was naive, or blissfully ignorant. But I got this idea in my head that people of colour could do anything they wanted to do. And careers were supposed to be fun, not functional. I wanted that for myself.

"I really want to do something creative." I continued.

"But what will you do with a degree in advertising?" mum asked, "How will you find work? You'd struggle."

"You don't get a degree in advertising." I mumbled.

"Huh?" My mum tried really hard to comprehend what I was saying.

"I'd go to advertising school and there's this really good one, the Red and Yellow School of Logic and Magic. I've read all about it, here look, it sounds so cool." I passed my mum a crumpled brochure I saved from Mrs Fig in English class.

"You don't get a degree?" My mum took the brochure to examine it a bit closer.

"You have to get a degree Leilah, you can't *not* have a degree, how will you get a good job?"

Today, in 2025, that may seem like a ridiculous statement. The world is different now. But back then I knew what she meant. I believed it too. Without a degree I wasn't sure what my future looked like, if I'd even get a job. As Coloured people, we don't make decisions the same way everyone else does. There are different elements at play, and there are things we need to consider that our White peers probably don't need to think about. Like choosing a career that'll guarantee financial security. We're trained to choose a career that's centred around money. Which path will help us get a high-paying job? Which path is a guaranteed track to success? Which path will enable us to earn money fast? Because money is everything if you grew up having none.

Mum continued to study the brochure. "What would you want to study at advertising school?"

I looked at the brochure in her hands already knowing the detail on every page from all the days that I've read it before. I knew there were two major branches in advertising: graphic design and copywriting. There it was again. Art. Staring at me in the face, telling me I couldn't have it. The course requirements said that you didn't need prior art experience, but it would be advantageous. *Advantageous*. Meaning without it I would be at a disadvantage.

"I would study copywriting," I said sheepishly. "You have a bigger range of jobs you can go into with copywriting, than graphic design."

My mum dashed out of my room and came back with the jobs section of today's newspaper.

"Yes you're right. Look here, there are loads more jobs for writers in the paper. Look, I only found one job for a graphic designer so far."

I nodded. Next to art and design, writing was something I really enjoyed and was actually good at. More importantly, I think it got my mum to look beyond a career in engineering for me. So I took the win.

Being the first grandchild in the family to get a tertiary education was a big deal. My mum wanted to get it right. She wanted me to be successful. But she also wanted me to be happy. My parents got married when they were both very young, in their early twenties. My mum was an executive assistant to a senior official in the government where she was treated like royalty. She left her job in the government when she had me, and never returned. Instead she took a job close to home, only four blocks away, at a retail clothing store selling discounted fashion. It was an awful looking building that had the aesthetics of a factory warehouse and she had a tyrant for a boss. Most days she was hauling boxes from the stockroom, organising the inventory according to season and sizes, and merchandising the mannequins in the store. On sale days she would work until 10pm in the evenings. I don't think she was ever happy there, but it allowed her to be close to me when I was a toddler, and that gave her a different kind of happiness. Being close to home gave her peace of mind that if she ever needed to get away from work for an emergency, she could.

I think my dad was a self-taught architect, a draughtsman. I'd always see him behind his makeshift desk in my parents' bedroom drawing complex lines and shapes on large sheets of transparent paper with fine liner pens — the pens I still have with me today. I always wanted to write with those pens, but I knew they were expensive so I shouldn't touch them. I don't know exactly what my dad's profession was before he met my mum and before I was born. I didn't know him that well. Or maybe even at all. I remember days of my dad floating in and out of the house, in and out of our lives. I remember vague and brief conversations, but I don't remember much from my childhood with my father. It was like he wasn't ever there, but I'm sure he was because I have this photo that I keep in my purse where he's holding me as a baby and he's laughing. He seemed happy about me being there. So maybe he was.

While my mum knew everything about me, I don't think my dad knew me that well. We lived in the same house as strangers. Conversations with him felt unnatural and strained. I never held eye contact. He never held eye contact. We rarely spoke. We existed in the same world. But not together. And yet there was not one specific incident that led to us being this way. Just a series of circumstances and continued scenarios that created a pattern where a father-daughter relationship couldn't naturally exist. I have very few memories of my dad from when I grew up. My memory bank is sparse. What's ingrained in my head are all the stories that my aunties have told me about him. But the few memories where I do remember him, they are vivid and traumatic.

There is one memory of my dad that I can't seem to forget. I was around 5 or 6 years old. My mum was at work. Ouma Dia was in the garden. My dad was doing one of his intricate drawings on the large white desk in my parents' bedroom. I stood over the desk watching with great interest.

I don't know what I did, but I remember him saying to me, in his nonchalant way, not with any violence or aggression. Just as plainly and softly in a very matter-of-fact way, while not even looking up from his architectural drawings,

"You don't care about me."

"I'm no one to you."

"I'm rubbish."

"I'm no one."

"Go. Go to your ouma."

I continued to stand there silently. Lonely tears streaming down my face. He looked up from his drawings and saw me crying silently. He dropped his drawings and picked me up and laughed apologetically, saying he didn't mean any of it, it was all just a joke.

Ouma came in from the garden and asked what was wrong. She carried me to the main house to watch cartoons with my great uncle, Amie Salie. I watched as Amie Salie cut perfectly straight lines out of dark, woven fabric. I later learned he was a tailor. It was customary for the men and women in our culture to occupy positions in the clothing industry in Cape Town. The skill and the knowledge of different fabrics was a legacy of

Malay slaves.

Ouma made us both a cup of sweet tea and Amie Salie showed me how to drink it out of a saucer. Amie Salie was the person who nurtured my imagination. He told me wild stories of fairies that floated through our garden and protected the fruit on the trees he planted for me. To this day the Cape Gooseberry is one of my favourite fruits. We called them appeliepies; in Britain it's called Physalis. It reminds me so much of my childhood and of Amie Salie. May his beautiful soul rest in peace.

When I was much younger he planted an appeliepie tree in the garden. Every season it would bear fruit. Bright orange balls hidden inside a delicate papery pod that was so fun to pick from the tree. Amie Salie told me it was the fairies' favourite fruit and as a child that fascinated me. It was magic. It was Amie Salie that taught my 5-year-old self that concepts can exist outside of your brain. That you can create realities from thoughts in your head. And maybe then, without me realising, was when I first fell in love with ideas.

Milo's daughter

In the halls of Livingstone high school, amidst the chatter of classmates and the clatter of books closing for the semester, excitement buzzed in the air. I reflected over my career decisions. The past year I particularly poured my heart into every word I wrote. Whether it was crafting essays for English class or scribbling poetry in the margins of my notebooks. Moreover, writing became my refuge, my sanctuary from the tumult of teenage life. As graduation loomed on the horizon, I found myself drawn to a path I didn't expect: Ad School, to become a copywriter.

"So, you're really going for it, huh?" my friend Sarah remarked one afternoon, her eyes sparkling with curiosity.

I nodded, a mixture of excitement and trepidation churning within me. "Yeah, I think it's what I'm meant to do."

"It suits you," she said with a grin. "I mean, you've always had a way with words," her words buoyed my spirits, washing away the doubts that had lingered at the edges of my mind.

As other friends chimed in with their own words of encouragement, I felt a sense of validation wash over me.

"I wish I had something I was that passionate about," Tash mused wistfully.

"You'll find it," I assured her, though my own confidence wavered slightly. "It's just a matter of time."

In those moments, surrounded by the support and camaraderie of my friends, I felt a sense of belonging unlike any I had experienced before. It made me feel better about missing out on five years of studying art at high school. Even though writing became a manufactured interest, hearing others' perspectives of my writing made me feel like I was meant to write. It made me feel like I belonged to the world of writing, and that writing belonged to me. And as I embarked on the next chapter of my journey, I carried with me the knowledge that writing was not just something I did, it was who I was meant to be.

* * *

It was the day before submissions closed for the Red & Yellow School of Logic and Magic. My mum handed me my ad concepts that she had printed out at the print shop nearby where she worked. We sat on the floor of my room and she helped me file the submissions in order to get it ready for the post office. One of the tasks was to create an ad for myself: an ad of why I should be accepted to the great school of advertising. My mum read it again and smiled.

"You're so good at this, really," she beamed with pride. "Can I show your dad?"

I continued sorting my application pack without saying anything.

She asked again, pointing to the ad for myself. "Just this one?"

"Okay."

I was 18 and never had a full conversation with my father in all of those 18 years. Not about school, not about my writing, not about the weather, not about what we had for dinner, not about anything. We might've spoken a few times asking each other if there was any soap or toothpaste, but other than that, I don't recall a meaningful conversation with him. It wasn't like that moment when he told me that I didn't care about him was some character defining moment, and I held a grudge or anything. There was just nothing there. A comfortable emptiness.

Letting my dad read my writing in my submission pack was weird. It was like opening myself up to a stranger. But I guess quite a few strangers would read the same piece when they reviewed my work, to decide if I was good enough for Ad School. So I thought, what the heck.

There were days when I thought about why I didn't have the same relationship with my dad that I had with my mum. I'd see him making his Cuppa Soup in the open plan kitchen, while I sat on ouma's red velvet sofa watching cartoons with my cousins. Cuppa Soup and two minute noodles were easy and affordable lunch items to get hold of while my mum worked at the retail store, so we had loads of that in the cupboards. My dad would drift through the house in his own world, not seeing anyone, not seeing me. He was an enigma. Apart from my mum, he was my closest living relative, and yet I was not part of his world.

Weeks after I submitted my application for Ad School, I started to wonder if I'll ever hear back. Graduation day was nearly upon us and I didn't have any back up schools or plans. I had picked the best advertising school in the country to apply to, the ivy league of Ad Schools, knowing full well that the school had never seen many applications from students of colour. Coloureds didn't go into creative industries. Coloureds went for sensible, sustainable careers. Here I was taking one shot to become a struggling artist. Moreover, the bar to get into Red & Yellow was high. There was no guarantee I'd even get in.

On a particularly mundane afternoon after school, my childhood friend Ani and I embarked on our ritual pilgrimage to the corner shop, the promise of 2-minute noodles and shared laughter spurring us forward. Our mums worked together at the retail shop; Ani and I became instant friends when we met at 3 years old. We grew up together and spent nearly every single day together. Ani was my closest confidant. With our pockets weighed down by spare change and our minds already drifting into the realm of snack-induced bliss, we strolled through the familiar streets of our neighbourhood. Then, with practised efficiency, we navigated the maze of aisles, our eyes scanning the shelves. Finally, we emerged triumphant, our hands clutching a colourful array of instant noodles in all their sodium-laden glory.

"Score!" Ani exclaimed.

I chuckled in agreement, my stomach already rumbling in anticipation. As we approached my house, a flash of colour caught my eye, a thick cream envelope adorned with a bold red and yellow circle splattered across its surface. It was addressed to me. With a sense of anticipation building in the pit of my stomach, I tore open the envelope, the sound of crinkling paper filling the room as I extracted its contents. And as I unfolded the letter nestled within, my heart skipped a beat, the words leaping off the page and searing themselves into my memory forever.

```
Dear Leilah

We're pleased to confirm your acceptance as a
copywriting student at the Red & Yellow School.
```

"Oh shit I actually got in.
   I got in!
   I got in! To AD SCHOOL!
   I GOT IN!
   I GOT IN!" I yelled.

My dad was the only other person home at the time. I saw him from the corner of my eye when I passed my parents' bedroom on my way to my room. But by then so many years have passed. So many moments have already been lost.

Our relationship reduced to little more than polite nods and obligatory exchanges. And like he put it in his own words one day, "Leilah is already grown up and it is too late now".

My father, a silent presence in the periphery of my consciousness, drifted through the house like a ghost, his presence both felt and ignored in equal measure. We only spoke to each other when we needed to. There was just nothing to say. No relationship. No feelings. Just a peaceful nothingness, with both of us expecting absolutely nothing from each other. But as he stood before me now, his presence a silent plea for connection, I felt a glimmer of hope stirring within me, a fragile thread of possibility weaving its way through the tapestry of our shared history.

"Did you get in, Leilah?" He inquired, his voice tentative yet hopeful.

"Yeah," I said as I held up the letter.

A smile tugged at the corners of his lips as he reached out to take the letter from my hands, his eyes scanning the words with a mixture of pride and admiration.

"Slamat!" he exclaimed, the Malay word for congratulations falling from his lips like a benediction.

"Wow, well done Leilah. This is really great," he said again while he read the words on my acceptance letter.

I never looked him in the eye. But I smiled when I looked

directly past his eyeline. There was a crusty brown wound drying up on his forehead. Dried blood. I'm immediately taken back to that one Saturday afternoon when we fetched my mum from work. She came out to say she'd be a minute as they needed to close up and prepare the store for the next day. My dad locked the car and went across the street to the taxi rank. I think he might have known someone who drove taxis.

As a side hustle between architecture, my dad installed sound systems for people. We'd see people with the most pimped-out cars pull up in the driveway to have their sound system installed. He became sort of notorious for this in our neighbourhood. A large part of his clientele were taxi drivers. They brought their taxis as well as their own personal cars to our house to have their sound pimped-out by my dad. They were not shady characters, just family men trying to make a living driving taxis. They knew me as Milo's daughter.

It was not unusual for him to know people at the taxi rank, where I saw him walk to. He sat on the metal railing talking to someone casually. Out of nowhere another man approached him, holding a loose piece of the metal railing. I watched as he swung the piece of metal at my dad's head. His head just swung to the other side as he caught his balance and got off the railing. I looked away pretending not to see anything as my dad got up and walked back to the car. My heart jumped right into my throat and it almost choked me.

Witnessing your father being beaten with a metal rod across the face is not something that leaves your memory easily. It stays with you year after year after year. Especially if you've not processed those emotions properly. My therapist says if you don't process trauma, you can't let it out, it stays inside. And it haunts you. I never told my mum what I saw that day. I learned from an early age that to deal with my own trauma, I need to turn inwards, towards myself, zombifying myself, pretending not to exist. If I didn't exist, even for a moment, it meant my feelings didn't exist and that would make them disappear. It numbed the shock and the pain, and became my coping mechanism.

My dad handed the letter back to me still smiling. I felt a sense of sympathy for him, as he tried to cover his wound that I also pretended not to see. I tried to understand the complexities of his life that might've led to that moment on the metal railing. His life that I had no part in, his life that I didn't know. I tried not to think about what situations he might have been exposed to, his personal struggles, what his life was like when I was growing up, why I never got to build a relationship with him. I let my thoughts float away, as I watched my dad disappear into my parents' bedroom again.

That evening I showed that letter to everyone in the house and we talked about it endlessly around the dinner table. Even after ouma Dia passed, we still held family nights in our family home. By then we'd moved homes and Amie Salie and aunty Weya had also passed away. I loved all of them dearly. But the most heartbreaking for me was seeing Amie Salie go from a jovial old man who lit up the room with his laughter and his dry humour to a skeletal bedridden shadow of his former self. Until eventually the cancer took him.

My mum insisted to uphold family night after we lost my grandmother, Amie Salie and Aunty Weya. And so every Friday night, my mum's two sisters and their families would come over for a big family supper. But not like that one you're probably picturing. Family nights at ours were loud and casual, we'd sit around the dark wooden kitchen table. We'd argue about what to have for supper every week and we'd always end up at the same place: Aneesas vienna and chip parcels. My dad would be there, but not at the table. He always ate supper alone in my parents' bedroom watching football. It was the norm, and no one bothered to question it. Why my dad never joined us for supper, or Sunday drives to the beach, or annual family picnics. Or any moment in my life, really.

At the table, I was careful not to get Aneesas all-sauce gatsby stains on my acceptance letter. It was my entry into the elite world of advertising, and I could not wait.

The school of logic and magic

[9]"Mowbrie Kaaaaaaaap!" shouted the gaachie who hung halfway out the window of the taxi. A South African taxi. Not an air-conditioned, leather-clad Uber Comfort, not a spacious London Black Cab with contactless pay inside the cabs, not even a yellow New York-style taxi. A South African taxi is a common means of transport in Cape Town. It's a 16-seater commuter minibus, sometimes referred to as kombis. You can catch them anywhere along the main road because they'll stop anywhere, and it very rarely seats 16 - most of the time there are up to 20 people in those taxis. The gaachie is the taxi assistant who calls for passengers and collects the money on a minibus taxi.

I despised sitting at the back of the taxi because you had to shout at the driver when you'd near your stop. If you didn't, they wouldn't stop. My mum and I sat in the first section near the sliding doors. The gaachie always climbed in and squeezed in on top of the other passengers; the gaachie never took up a

---

[9] A named taxi route that would stop at major destinations like, Mowbrie (Mowbray) through to Kaap (Cape Town city). Similarly, in London, "this is a Northern Line service to Battersea Power Station"

seat because a seat was money. Today, his elbow was resting on my knee, as he knelt on the floor screaming out the window, "Claremont, Mowbrie Kaaaaaap!"

I sat there, taking in the whiffs of 20 people's body odour, excited for the day ahead. Not once throughout that uncomfortable ride did I wish I was someone driving next to the taxi with their parents in their SUVs. I was too amped. We were going to see where my career in advertising was about to start; a meet and greet with the founders at the Red & Yellow School.

I stumbled out of the taxi when we reached our stop in Woodstock. An old, industrial style building with a big sign on the front that told us we were in the right place.

"Hi, can I help you?" The receptionist's voice rang out, cutting through the air before we even reached the desk.

"Hello, we're here to get a tour of the school," my mother replied, her voice carrying a hint of the posh accent she reserved for such occasions, a subtle indicator of our unfamiliarity in these settings.

"Sorry, we don't do public tours," the receptionist responded, her tone cool and dismissive.

"My daughter was accepted at the school for next year. We have an appointment for a tour today," my mother explained, her demeanour poised and composed despite the setback.

The receptionist's expression softened as she glanced at me

and then back at my mother. "Oh, my apologies! Of course, come have a seat! I'll get the guys."

"Leilah! Mrs. Adams!" one of them called out warmly. "Welcome to the Red & Yellow School."

"Thank you! Leilah's very excited to be here," my mother responded, her accent still present as she exchanged pleasantries with the men.

I smiled and shook their hands, feeling a surge of anticipation coursing through me as we prepared to embark on our tour. As we traversed the corridors, my eyes moved from one poster to the next, taking in the witty one liners and impeccable art direction on the ad concepts that lined the walls. I was in awe. Taken aback. I was witnessing pure, unregulated creativity and for the first time ever, I felt like I could belong somewhere.

"Work from our students," one of the men said smiling. He must have noticed my jaw hanging on the floor of the corridor. I just smiled in response. I was even more socially awkward and introverted at 18 and therefore didn't say much. I'm realising that more and more as I recollect these moments to tell this story.

We entered a room filled with vinyls and CDs which was the music library where students chose the songs to use for the TV ads that they made. They told me about the process of making an ad, how your first draft is never your finished product, how you'll get feedback from your fellow students and your lecturers, how you'll need to be thick-skinned to take on the feedback because that's what the ad industry is about. They told me about an example where a lecturer had the student's work on the floor and pretended to vomit on it, and the student's second version of that work ended up winning an award for the school. They wanted me to know that this school produced talent. Not just any talent, talent that would go on to work for big creative agencies and win awards. I was beaming. I wanted all of it.

The only thing we needed to do to confirm my acceptance was pay the deposit, which was half of the annual tuition fees for the year: R30 000 (£1500). In 2002, this was a small fortune for my mum. It was more than what she got paid annually at the clothing store where she worked. It was a shock to my mum, but she handled the situation with grace.

"Yes of course! We'll do an electronic transfer as soon as we get home." My mum managed to say.

We didn't do the transfer. We obviously couldn't, my mum didn't have that kind of money. We tried to get a bursary. But as it turned out, advertising was a specialist course, certainly not a necessity in the country. It was not medicine or engineering, where there were hundreds of organisations set up to offer bursaries to underprivileged students who wanted a career in that field of study. It was just advertising. In those days, bursaries for advertising didn't exist, because the students entering the field, typically privileged, rarely needed financial help. For weeks my mum tried to raise the money so that I could go to my dream school, but it just wasn't enough. I knew the ongoing fees, the books and art supplies I'd need every year would just multiply. It would cripple her financially. It was just not feasible. Somehow that career in engineering with a full bursary and a job lined up at the end of it didn't seem so bad. If only I had the grades to get in.

The deadline to confirm acceptance at the Red & Yellow School passed and I was faced with accepting that I wouldn't be going to Ad School after all. We did find a good second choice though. My mum enrolled me in a Journalism course at Varsity College, which was expensive too but just about doable with a personal loan. The fact that you got a Diploma from a recognised higher education body made my mum feel more secure about this decision too. Enrolling in the Journalism course required a significant financial investment. It was a precarious balancing act for my mum, one that required careful budgeting, sacrifice, and having to ask family members for money. I hate that she had to put herself in that situation. This was something I was blissfully unaware of at the time. My mum protected me from this, never told me about her financial struggles because she said it was none of my business as a child.

Sure, I wouldn't get the support from Ad School to help me land a job in the advertising world, but I would receive copywriting training from a recognised institution. I knew breaking into advertising without formal Ad School training would be challenging. However, with a journalism diploma, I was confident I could do it. No problem.

Then the world turned digital

~ 2004 ~

Varsity College was a small business school, a two-storey campus, set behind the main road of Rosebank in Cape Town. The classes were much smaller than I was used to at high school; there were only 15 people in all my lectures. I was one of only a few people of colour in my class. The campus had a small tuck shop that served sandwiches and snacks during breaks, and a cosy outdoor eating area that could seat about 30 people at one time. In contrast to Red and Yellow's industrial creative space with posters all along the walls, Varsity College's walls were more clean cut and minimalistic. It felt more like a corporate office, than a place to learn and be inspired. Not the way Red & Yellow felt.

Journalism was an interesting course. I learned about writing for different media, investigative journalism, news rooms, creative writing and digital content production. Those years, spent in those spacious classrooms with my small group of peers were some of the best years of my life. We didn't make ads but we made magazines and built websites and learnt about blogging and digital copywriting. I learnt so much about online content creation in that course, something I didn't get much exposure to at school. Mainly because we didn't have computers at school. My lecturer kept telling us how content would be online in the next ten years, and that digital media was the future. The year was 2004 and I didn't believe him. I couldn't grasp the concept of everything being online when analogue was so beautiful. So expressive. So real.

But I gave it a shot. I enjoyed creating digital magazines, customising my own blog for class and documenting my every day. Being anonymous on the internet became something I was quite good at. As an introvert, being anonymous on the world wide web came naturally to me. And when Twitter launched, I was all over it. My lecturer encouraged spending our time writing online; he called my class the future digital content creators of the world. I definitely still wanted to make ads, but this new medium, micro blogging, where I could publish words, uncensored and unfiltered, intrigued me. Online, I could be anyone I wanted. So I decided to be a dreamer, rocker, writer with a link to my blog and my MySpace page. I used an anime picture that only slightly looked like me for my profile photo. And that's when I first delved into the world of social media, where anyone could be a publisher. Maybe my lecturer was onto something, I thought.

Paying for my education was extremely difficult for my mum. She never mentioned this to me, in fact she did everything to hide it from me. She used her own name and the house as collateral to get a personal loan approved, in order to get me the money to go to Varsity College. It took me way too long to realise the enormous gesture this was from my mum, when I noticed that all my friends had student loans to pay off, and I had none. She always said that children didn't ask to be in this world, and that it was a parent's job to give their children everything they needed in order to succeed. There were months when she thought she couldn't pay my fees, then my dad would sell some of his tools and anything he owned to help my mum with my tuition fees. Sometimes they'd still come up short. To this day, I honestly don't know how my mum managed to pay my school fees and how I was able to graduate without missing a semester. Without being pulled from class due to missed payments.

While I was working towards my diploma, I needed to earn money too. My mum was the only one working to pay the mortgage and put food on the table. My dad's income was not consistent. And as the world turned digital, he stopped doing his architectural drawings. He got an old laptop from his friend and started learning AutoCAD, but I don't think it went anywhere. There were days and nights when I didn't see my dad at all. I don't know where he went or what he did but I didn't ask questions. We were not the type of family to talk about important things.

It was customary for my mum to pretend that everything was normal in front of me. It mattered to her that I had a normal upbringing. And so I started playing along. I existed in this world where chaos would happen around me, but my body didn't know how to react. My initial reaction would be to use the only coping mechanism I knew: to zombify myself and just carry on with life as if everything was normal. I wouldn't react; I wouldn't even blink. I retreated even deeper into myself as I got older.

But I couldn't always keep it together, and so one day I only slightly broke out of character. It was a Spring afternoon. I remember because the sky was a soft turquoise blue with scattered clouds, and the breeze from the car window was cool on my face. We drove to my mum's younger sister's house. I was sitting in the backseat of the car my dad drove that day. Zahier agreed that I could use his computer for a college project. My mum and dad were arguing in the front about something that, for the life of me, I can't remember what it was. I was distracted. My mum was screaming at my dad to stop the car. He stopped the car, she got out and she wanted to walk the rest of the way to my aunt's house. It was only a few kilometres from where we stopped on the side of the highway.

My mum's voice pierced through the air, "Leilah, get out of the car!"

I stayed frozen in my seat, my heart pounding.

My dad turned on my mum, his face red with anger. "You don't care about me!" he yelled, his voice cracking.

"She doesn't speak to me!" His eyes were wild with pain.

"She doesn't love me!" His gaze shifted to me, and I felt a knot tighten in my chest. "You're the reason she doesn't love me!" he accused, pointing a trembling finger at my mum.

I sat on the backseat, tears streaming down my face. I didn't say anything to tell him that it wasn't true. Because we didn't talk about these things in our family. And we didn't say I love you. So I didn't say it. It felt a little like that day in front of my dad's desk, where he told six-year-old me that I didn't love him. I didn't get out of the car. I didn't know why I was crying. I didn't know why they were arguing. I didn't want to walk from the highway to my aunt's house.

My mum got back in the car, and we continued the drive to my aunt's house in silence. Once there, I sat at Zahier's computer, trying to focus on my project while tears dripped onto the keyboard.

"It's okay," he said softly. "Don't worry about it."

Like I belonged in this wealthy world of college

In the summer, I embarked on a new adventure, taking up a part-time job at the vibrant Claremont flea market, where I specialised in creating intricate henna tattoos. The shop was a kiosk, in a small summer street market, and it was a kaleidoscope of colours and characters, each day offering a new story. Bojan, the enigmatic and kind-hearted owner of the tattoo shop, took me under his wing. With his patient guidance, I learned the delicate art of mixing the perfect shade of black henna and the precise techniques needed to apply it flawlessly using intricate stencils. What started as a tentative effort soon became second nature, and before long, I could craft detailed designs with my eyes closed.

This job was more than just work; it was an immersion into a world where art met the everyday lives of fascinating people. The shop was a lively social hub, a crossroads where people from all walks of life converged. Some came in seeking the perfect tattoo to adorn their skin, while others were drawn to the warmth and camaraderie that Bojan's shop exuded. It was a place where stories were exchanged, friendships were forged, and the air was always thick with laughter and creativity. One of the people I met there was MJ, my husband.

I made a lot of money just doing tattoos for people. I guess now, I'd argue that a lot was actually a little, but when you had no money before and you start earning something, then a lot seems significant in comparison to nothing at all.

Before long, Bojan's restless creativity led him to suggest a new venture: crafting name-on-a-rice-grain necklaces. This intricate art form required a steady hand and an eye for detail. Bojan, ever the patient mentor, showed me how to delicately hold each tiny grain of rice with tweezers and inscribe names using an ultra-fine tip pen, reminiscent of the ones my father used for his meticulous architectural drawings. Once the names were elegantly penned onto the minuscule grains, we carefully placed each one into a tiny vial of clear liquid, sealing it securely before affixing it to a necklace chain.

The process was both painstaking and fascinating, and soon I found myself deeply engrossed in this new craft. Bojan's shop became even more of a magnet for curious customers, each eager to own a piece of personalised, wearable art. On quieter days, Bojan encouraged me to create as many necklaces as I wished for myself, allowing my creativity to run wild. On the bustling days when our booth was swarmed with eager patrons, Bojan meticulously counted the day's earnings, ensuring that my efforts were duly recognised and rewarded. Every evening, he paid me my salary with a sense of fairness that was rare to find. Then, in an unexpected and generous gesture, he split the profits with me equally.

"You bring the people to the shop," he would say, his eyes twinkling with appreciation. "You deserve to share in the success."

Though I was initially taken aback by his generosity, I accepted it gratefully, recognising the unique bond and mutual respect that had formed between us.

I gave my mum some of the money I made at the tattoo shop. I put some away to pay for travel to college and lunch money. My mum was immensely grateful for the money, even though I don't think it made much of a difference to all the bills she needed to pay. Sometimes she'd lean in and ask with a warm smile, "Do you have any small change for your dad?"

"Mm-hmm," I'd reply, nodding as I handed her a few more notes to pass along to him.

"You should give it to him yourself. It would mean so much more coming from you," she'd encourage, her eyes sparkling with a mix of wisdom and tenderness.

And so I'd walk into my parents' bedroom where my dad was watching football, and I said nothing. I just stood there looking at him and reached out my hand with a few notes.

He looked at the money in my hand and asked, "Wow, are you sure, Leilah? Can you afford this?"

At first, he refused to take the money, his brow furrowed with concern. But I insisted, my resolve firm as I assured him that I could afford it and that it was meant for him.

"Yeah, it's fine," I said, pressing the notes into his hand.

"Thank you so much," he replied, his voice tinged with gratitude as he finally accepted the money.

And so, this little ritual became our monthly charade, a heartfelt exchange that repeated each time I got paid.

What I really wanted to say was "Stop doing jobs where you'd get hurt. Stay home with us." But I knew that the R300 (£15) that I gave him then probably wouldn't last long. Instead, I hoped that my silence would speak volumes, that he'd understand the unspoken plea behind my gesture. Having access to money gave me some form of independence. I was able to order frozen yoghurt after class at college with my friends, instead of pretending I was too full to have any. I was able to go out with my friends on weekends without having to ask my mum for the little money she had. I didn't want to be the type of person where money controlled me. But I couldn't help notice the difference that having money made. Like saying yes to more things, instead of being restricted because of having no money. I was able to be more me around people who had more than I had. No one suspected that I didn't have money. My fair complexion, jet black hair cut into shoulder-length uneven layers made me look rebellious. And in those years rebellious punks were the aesthetic of the rich kids at Varsity College.

Here I was, yet again, the poorest one in my friends circle.

It was a direct symptom of my mum wanting more for me, pushing for more for me, getting me into institutions where I shouldn't naturally be. The descendant of a slave. The daughter of a saleslady and a part-time architect/sound system installer/jack of all trades. And yet I never felt poor. My mum always made a plan to protect me from those feelings, ensuring I remained blissfully ignorant.

In my second year as a Journalism student, I signed up to work on the college magazine. I needed a camera to take photographs for the features we published. I also needed to be present at college events to provide editorial coverage for the magazine. The events were always after college and into the evenings, which meant taking a taxi or the metrorail was out of the question, even if my mum travelled with me. But my mum didn't want me to miss out on the opportunity of being part of the production of the magazine, so she'd beg and borrow lifts from everyone she knew. She also asked her friends if I could borrow their cameras to cover the events. Her friends handed over their expensive cameras to this teenager going to a raucous college event, without a second thought. Every. Single. Time. My mum had really good friends.

One evening, my dad came home with a metallic blue Sony Cybershot 1.3. megapixel digital camera. It was a second-hand camera that he got from one of his friends but it was in working order. He gave it to me. It gleamed under the dim light of our living room, a modest yet significant gift that held the promise of new beginnings.

"How much was it? Where did you get it?" My mum's voice

rang out, a mix of curiosity and concern.

"She needs it for college. Now she won't have to borrow anyone's cameras any more," my dad replied, his tone carrying a hint of pride in his resourcefulness.

"Thank you," I uttered softly, my heart swelling with gratitude as I accepted the camera. It was a gesture of support that transcended words, a symbol of my father's belief in my aspirations.

I retreated to my room, cradling the camera in my hands. It was a second-hand treasure, but to me, it was priceless. With eager fingers, I inserted batteries scavenged from my CD player's remote and hunted for a spare memory card. As the camera powered on, its digital display flickered to life, a beacon of possibility in my hands.

I spent hours exploring its functions, navigating through menus and experimenting with different settings. Each click of the shutter filled me with a sense of empowerment, a tangible connection to my passion for photography.

In the days that followed, the camera became an extension of myself, a faithful companion on my journey through college and beyond. It accompanied me to lectures and outings, bearing witness to the moments that defined my experience. With each snapshot, I captured fragments of my reality, weaving them into a visual tapestry of memories. As the year unfolded, I filled scrapbooks with printed photographs, each page a testament to the adventures I embarked on and the lessons I learned. Through the lens of my camera, I found my voice, a means of expression that transcended the confines of words alone.

Having my own creative tools levelled the playing field, empowering me to chart my own course and embrace the journey ahead with newfound confidence. And though I never found the words to express it, the camera my dad gifted me became a symbol of love, support, and the boundless possibilities that lay ahead. I never told my dad how much it meant to me.

My family wasn't exactly poor, we just weren't as wealthy as the people I went to college with. This camera, though battered and second-hand, was a statement of wealth for me. And I think somehow my dad knew that. He saw the school I went to, the events he sometimes drove me to, the friends houses he dropped me off at. Somehow, in his own way, even though he couldn't support me financially, I think he wanted to help me on this big journey to ad land. My mum had her own way of helping me feel like I belonged in this wealthy world of college. She used to dress me in the best clothes from the samples she found at the retail store where she worked. Every year she used her bonus to buy me a pair of Converse or Nike's, whatever I chose. It didn't matter what you wore, but if your shoes were expensive, it was hard to tell that you didn't come from money. The people I went to college with knew that people with less money than them existed, but they didn't often realise that they might be sharing a classroom with them. Rich people usually expect everyone around them to have money, so it was actually very easy to blend in and let them make the assumptions that I was one of them. The camera, the clothes and the shoes made it a little bit easier for me to blend in.

Public transport

~ 2005 ~

In my final year of college my classes shifted from afternoons to mornings. This meant that I could take up more hours at the Bojan's tattoo shop after college. Varsity College was in Rondebosch and the flea market was in Claremont which was just two stops in the other direction on the metrorail. The route passed through a predominantly White neighbourhood which meant I would be safe.

In the mornings I got ready for college at the same time as my mum got ready for work. We'd walk down to the corner of Essex Road and my mum would wave her hand up to catch a taxi. The store where she worked was only a few minutes walk from where the taxi stopped and behind the taxi rank was Wynberg train station, where I'd catch the train to Rondebosch for college. I'd usually meet Roz from class at the station and we travelled to college together. For this reason only, my mum finally allowed me to travel on my own. Even though the Southern Line route was relatively safe - Wynberg, Kenilworth, Harfield Road, Claremont, Newlands, Rondebosch - my mum still had some reservations about me on the metrorail.

Cars were a luxury not everyone could afford at the time. Studying and paying for a driving licence test was also a privilege that not everyone could afford. That was reserved for people who had money and who had their own cars to practice their driving on. Taxis were the general mode of transport for most people of colour. The buses were safer, but the bus routes didn't always intersect with the areas where we needed to go. The metrorail came with its own set of problems. Even after apartheid fell, the trains were still segregated into first and third class. During apartheid, first-class carriages were reserved for White passengers, while third-class sat at the back of the train, the section that had once been designated for non-Whites. I have no idea why there was no second class. I never asked.

Today, if you wanted to sit in front of the train you could buy a first class ticket, but they were almost triple the price of third class tickets. It was a tactic designed to keep people of colour in third class carriages even in a post-apartheid South Africa. Most of us couldn't afford first class tickets and would cram into the back of the train with a third class ticket. And sometimes you just had to go by taxi because there were no routes on the bus or train that would take you to your destination. The taxi experience, though cheaper than the train, is not for the faint-hearted. The worst of it being on the taxi rank, the place where taxis park while filling up with passengers before they commence their route. There were no signs, you just had to listen to what the gaachie was shouting to know where each taxi would be going.

The gaachie always shouted the most repugnant things at

people while the taxi was stationary, waiting to fill up. All the big-boned women needed to sit at the back of the taxi. Only one big-boned woman per row was allowed, because if two women of the same size sat next to each other then you couldn't fit four people on a seat. That was their logic. If you were a pretty girl with pin-straight hair you needed to sit in front, next to the driver or next to the gaachie. My mum tried to shield me from this abuse as much as she could by always travelling with me if I needed to take a taxi. This is why I never travelled alone. One morning my mum and I took the taxi from Essex Road corner and it was already quite full, so we had to squeeze in. The gaachie had his armpit directly in my face. I looked over at my mum and I could tell she sensed the irritation on my face. But she was powerless because there was nothing she could do. This was all part of the experience of riding in a taxi.

"Please could you move your arm out of my personal space?" I asked the gaachie.

The entire minibus filled with people turned to look at me. Did I say something wrong? I thought. I looked over at my mum and the expression on her face indicated that she was dying inside because she couldn't predict what would happen next.

"Oh, sorry." The gaachie told me and moved his arm out of my face.

My mum's face unclenched. Afterward, when we eventually got to our destination, she told me how surprised and proud she was of me in that moment. In all her life of travelling by taxi, she, like many others, were conditioned to accept this rough treatment. She'd never seen or heard anyone standing up for themselves in a taxi before. She said it would never have crossed her mind to say anything in a situation like that. It was just something you needed to endure as a downtrodden, second-class citizen in South Africa. If you were Coloured or Black you couldn't complain about anything and you needed to be grateful that you even had taxi fare or transport to take you where you needed to be. And here I was, a Coloured girl in Cape Town, going against the grain of what we were supposed to do. Using my voice and standing up for myself in the new South Africa.

I heard stories of my mum being an anti-apartheid protester when she was a teenager and just before she had me in 1985. I heard how she rioted in the streets with other people of colour. I heard how she and ouma Dia would block the vents and the bottom of the doors with towels to prevent the tear-gas from entering the house when I was a baby. I heard how she ran away from the police during a riot and she jumped from the third floor of the Golden Acre shopping centre to the ground floor just to get away from them with their guns, chasing after Coloured and Black teenagers in school uniform. Teenagers who were fighting for equality in South Africa.

During the apartheid period, people of colour couldn't attend private schools. Model C Schools with better facilities and learning programs were reserved for White students. People of colour were also not allowed to attend university or apply for any skilled work, thus forcing people into making a living as a trades-person. And even then, people of colour were paid less than their White counterparts. Other ridiculous apartheid rules included not being able to use public toilets that were labelled "Whites Only". People of colour had to go everywhere with their ID and had curfews so were not allowed out at night after curfew. All of Cape Town's beautiful blue flag beaches were off limits to people of colour. The Coloured generation before me also weren't allowed to make friends with or interact with people of different races. And because they couldn't vote in the general election, activism became the only way to raise your voice against inequality, and to stand up to the government.

Learning about these injustices my parents, grandparents and all non-White South Africans had to live through, I understand the choices that my mum made for me when I was growing up. Moving mountains to get me accepted at a good school in a White community, advocating for me to go to university, trying to persuade me to study science or engineering. All basic things that she didn't have access to when she was my age. I owe everything I am today to my mum, and others like her, who fought for the freedom of people of colour in South Africa. If it weren't for her, I would be writing a very different story right now.

Why do you keep you White?

At the age of 18, and as a child of the post-apartheid era, I can't say that I've experienced harsh racism. I guess I was shielded. Or sheltered. Having a different colour skin to everyone around me was never something that made me feel uncomfortable. Apartheid ended in 1990 when Nelson Mandela became the president of South Africa. I was born in 1985. I was about 5 years old when the regime fell and therefore have no recollection of it. The only time I'd notice that I was different was when someone else pointed it out to me.

Sometimes I'd bring friends home from college and my aunts would comment on how all my friends were White. They'd smile excitedly and look at me in awe having very normal conversations with my friends. I guess seeing me with my White friends was still novel to them, coming from a world where they were kept segregated all those years. I got it. Through their eyes, they could see the new generation of South Africans, the new generation of Coloured South Africans with new opportunities in a new South Africa. We were the future that they fought for all those years.

Meanwhile I was blending into this new world like I was born in it. I guess it helped that I was already quite fair-skinned and so all the prejudices that came with being darker-skinned like my mum, didn't really impact me. If anything, I didn't really feel like I fit in with any of my Coloured friends. They listened to R&B and hip hop, while I preferred punk rock music. They dressed in padded puffer coats and Buffalo's while I preferred ripped denim and Chuck Taylor's. The moment I graduated high school and had saved up enough money from the money mum gave me at weekends, I got my lip pierced in the exact same spot as Tom DeLonge's had his pierced. Blink 182 was all I'd listen to for months and months on end. Today, when I listen to the song *Stay Together For The Kids* I am immediately transported back to my old room in our family home with the bright pink wardrobe and my name graffiti'ed in pink and silver spray paint across my bedroom wall. A mural done for me by some of Cape Town's infamous taggers. I won't out you here.

I was the result of what a Coloured person could become in the free South Africa, without any racial limitations. And because of the new world I was exposed to, at college and the tattoo shop, I had become punk. Though I'd like to credit my love for punk and anarchy to my mum, being the original rebel as an anti-apartheid protestor. Still, I was a walking paradox. And to my Coloured community, I was a coconut: white on the inside and brown on the outside. I became used to the snide comments about me like "why do you keep you white?" or "sy wil soos die wittes wees" (she wants to be White) as soon as I entered a room.

When I met MJ, a Coloured boy who was into the same music

I was into and dressed the same way I did, it was like I met a unicorn. Another paradox. He walked up to the tattoo shop in the flea market one day. He was wearing faded blue jeans and a black formal shirt. A chunky silver chain hung out from the side of his jeans. Leather cuffs with silver studs on his wrists, not too different to the cuffs I wore every day.

"Hey," he said as he approached the tattoo shop.

"Hi"

"Where did you get your arm bands?" he asked.

"Oh, from Space Station. Inside the mall." I pointed in the direction of Cavendish Square. He said okay and walked away.

Later I learned that he wanted to ask for my number that day but was too intimidated. He came back the next day pretending he wanted a tattoo. And the rest, as they say, is history.

It was easy being myself around MJ. He understood me in a way that few people did. We made mix tapes together. We discovered new music together. We went to gigs together, all the while being the only people of colour in a mosh pit of whiteness. People said we were trying to be White, following White culture. The Coloured community thought it was because I still felt inadequate being Coloured; being myself. On the contrary, this so-called White culture felt more authentic to me than anything else. I loved punk rock with all my heart. As someone whose identity was shaped by being a mutt in society, not White nor Black, I somehow felt seen in the punk scene. I identified with the grit of drums and thrashing guitars a whole lot more than I could ever relate to smooth soulful rounded sounds of reggae and bass — a more acceptable preference of music for Coloured people. I couldn't help that the things that interested me happened to be White culture.

Punk also gave me a home when my own home felt chaotic. And boy, did my home feel chaotic all the time — there was never steady ground. My dad had storms inside him, while my mum did everything she could to shield me. Sometimes our living room felt less like a family home and more like a halfway house, with relatives and friends drifting in and out, never the same faces for long. Stability was foreign to me. What I did know, though, was the sound of raised voices, the shadows of fights, the sight of my dad returning battered from days and nights spent who knows where. So when the noise got too loud inside those walls, I found quiet in noise of another kind: the raw, unapologetic chaos of punk. That scene became my anchor, my compass when the one I was born into spun wildly. It was a place where people like us, the misfits of society, kids carrying bruises from homes, from schools, from the world that refused to accept them as they were, could come together and just scream. The youthful rebellion, anti-establishment attitudes, the confrontational fashion that says I don't give a F, is how we expressed ourselves.

And in those sweaty basements and cramped venues, angst wasn't something to be hidden or smoothed over — it was the very language that bound us together. Punk was always more than the music for me.

Class of 2005

On the evening of my graduation, my dad drove us to the venue. It was at a grand hotel on the Cape Town Foreshore; I could smell the ocean as we entered the parking area. We entered the foyer and I was escorted to a dressing room where all the graduates had their capes, hats and ribbons fitted. I spent most of the evening in that room on the plush velvet chairs catching up with my old classmates, while my mum, dad and MJ dined in the family area. They were serving light snacks on sticks and drinks on poseur tables, and called it cocktail hour.

When the program started, we took our seats in the auditorium. I sat with my class in the front of the room and my mum, dad and MJ sat somewhere towards the middle. The keynote speaker took the stage to kick off the evening. To this day, I still remember his words to us on that night.

"If in life you ever find yourself feeling down, because there will be moments where you will feel this way, just go outside and look up." He said this while stretching his arms like an eagle's wings beside him, tilting his head backwards to look up at the arched ceiling of the auditorium. "It's impossible not to feel happiness when you're looking up at the sky."

He was right. And to this day, when my anxiety flares up, I still go outside, stretch my arms out wide beside me and look up at the London sky. The relief is instant, and I always come back from that experience feeling like a new person. I think it has something to do with perspective. The sky is so vast, you can almost imagine planet Earth in the universe orbiting with all the other planets. And on Earth, somewhere in my corner of the world, I was just a tiny speck. My thoughts are even tinier than the tiny speck I take up on the globe. In an anxiety flare up, my thoughts feel big and all-consuming; I am suffocated by anxiety. But if my thoughts are so small in reality, it simply can't hold all the power that I think it does. The change in perspective is why this tactic works.

After the keynote, the dean of the college said some words too. Then came the moment that we'd all been waiting for. The dean called our names in alphabetical order. As she made her way through the list, my chest started bubbling with nerves. When my name was called, I heard a faint cheer from the middle of the room. I entered stage left, shook the dean's hand as she congratulated me and posed for the photograph with my diploma in my hand. Two minutes of grandeur that was over in a flash. After the last name was called and we were all back in our seats in the front row, the dean made a closing statement.

"Congratulations to the class of 2005."

150 graduation caps catapulted into the air above us as the

auditorium echoed with applause. We made it. The graduates of 2005. And the first of ouma Dia's grandchildren to graduate.

A Diploma in Journalism

~ 2006 ~

With my Diploma in Journalism, I couldn't wait to start making real ads, working on real briefs for real brands. I had so many ideas.

An internet cafe opened up in Wynberg a few months ago. It was modest; an old takeaway shop in the main street converted to a row of cubicles that housed a few computers. They charged R5 (24 pence) for 30 minutes of internet access. That's where I spent my mornings for the next few weeks, searching for my big break into advertising. With the launch of Bizcommunity and other online job boards it became easier to find available jobs in the advertising and marketing industry. Easier than before, when my mum used to scroll the jobs section of the newspaper.

I sent my shiny new CV to all and every opportunity in ad land, every ad agency that was looking to hire copywriters. My mum's middle sister had an office job in the HR and payroll industry, so any free time she had at work she dedicated to searching jobs for me.

There were so many jobs listed every single day for copywriters without any experience. Surely one of them would want to hire me, or at the very least, speak to me? But the response I got? Crickets. Was I doing something wrong?

It was already months after graduation and my peers from Class of 2005 had mostly started working already. Junior writer at the Argus, the major newspaper in the country. Radio producer at 5fm, the country's hit radio station. Editorial assistant at Elle magazine.

"How about you, Leilah?"

"Nothing yet, but I'm still looking."

Days turned into weeks that turned into months without a job. Meanwhile, everyone around me was getting hired. I felt confused. Frustrated. Angry.

"Why can't I get a job?" I asked MJ one Saturday afternoon on our way to Mc Donald's.

"You will," he said.

"I've been applying for almost two years! No one wants to hire me. Why not?!"

"It hasn't been two years. It's just a year and a bit. And you went into this specialist industry where it's not as easy to get a job."

I knew what he said was true. But I didn't want to hear it.

"My friends from college are all working already!" I yelled.

"You'll get your big break, just have patience." He said, dropping the last three words to a mumble.

Without a job and lack of income, I went back to the tattoo shop for a while. But the summer was over and even Bojan had lost interest in keeping the shop open. So I applied for another unpaid internship. I figured more experience couldn't hurt. Before I graduated, I spent two months working at a small digital content agency who produced content for SkySports. I didn't write for SkySports per se, but I wrote articles for their entertainment arm which was mostly about celeb news and the latest movies. It was a blog and they let me run with the content. The internship was a requirement in order to get my Diploma, but the college gave me no support in landing the internship the way Ad Schools do. The internship was a favour. My maternal cousin had a cousin from the other side of the family who worked in Journalism. He was the only person of colour I knew who had a career in writing. And not even a starving career; he had a full-blown successful career in writing. He was the editor of a popular sports magazine and he had a ton of influence in the industry. He made a call and got me the internship for two months. He gave me hope for myself, that I too would one day become as successful as he was. It often crossed my mind to call in another favour with him, but I didn't want to put him in an awkward position. I continued to strike out on my own.

Applying for a second, unpaid internship was a last resort. I thought if I had more experience to add to my CV, I would be more employable. They were also the only people who responded to my flood of applications.

The internship was for an indie surf magazine based in Bloubergstrand, one of the beachy neighbourhoods in Cape Town. For my interview, my mum and I arranged to take a taxi there together. I could hear the waves crash from inside the taxi as we drove through the main road, with the ocean on our left. The air was crisp, the smell of salt in the air and the sea a perfect duck egg grey. This would be a great place to come to work everyday. But how would I realistically get here everyday?

The building was on the beachfront, it had a media vibe to it with surfboards stacked at the entrance. I walked inside while my mum waited for me outside the building. I straightened my shirt and checked my reflection in the elevator mirror just before it stopped on the 7th floor. The editor of the features department met me at the elevators and led me through a tired looking office space to a small meeting room with two chairs. We spoke for 30 minutes about my education, my interests and my previous internship; the only work experience I had. An internship could lead to a permanent position if I performed well enough. And this was Cape Town's biggest surf magazine. Surf culture was adjacent to skate culture which was adjacent to the punk rock scene. This was my scene, my people. I was all in.

"Why would you want to do another internship?" the editor asked me.

"Well I feel like I need more experience and I really like this magazine." I replied.

"Okay, well, we'll let you know." He said as he thanked me for coming in.

He didn't let me know. And after several weeks of waiting for an answer, I took the hint that I didn't in fact get that internship. It was time to go back to the drawing board. Or for me, back to the internet cafe where I searched for jobs, applied for jobs, and waited for responses. Trying to find a job was becoming a full-time job and required a certain type of resilience that I did not possess. I wanted to give up many times. I nearly lost focus. Eventually, I started widening my applications and applied for any type of job in the industry, even roles outside of my specialism, copywriting. The only requirement: a paying salary.

Fang, the border collie

~ 2006 ~

In the summer of 2006, I got my first job offer for an SEO copywriter at an online marketing startup called Allura. It was one of many companies I hit on my job search marathon. I had no idea what SEO was but it had the word copywriter in the title so I went for it. It was also the only offer that came after 15 months of "Dear Hiring Manager" on repeat. The interview process was fast. The company was run by one woman, a digital marketing specialist who had gone and started her own firm, and it operated from her home in Vredehoek. It was there where I learned that SEO was an acronym for Search Engine Optimisation, a concept I never knew existed and one I had very little interest in.

I spent my days writing 500-word (or longer) articles for clients who wanted their websites to appear higher on Google. SEO, or Search Engine Optimisation, is the practice of improving a website's ranking in search results so more people find it. Since most people use Google to discover content, ranking higher on the search results page means more visitors to a website. I wrote content based on keywords that an SEO strategist had chosen for each client. For example, if the keyword was "secure gate," I had to include it several times in an article about gates. This way, when someone searched for "secure gates," our client's site would appear near the top. Most days it would be trying to plug in *"secure gate"* or another most searched term at least four times in an article I'd written. We were manufacturing relevance and there was nothing creative about it.

Allura and its founder taught me all the foundational knowledge about the online marketing industry, specifically the search engine marketing industry. I knew that it wasn't where I wanted to be. But I knew that I needed to gain experience in order to get where I wanted to be and this job gave me that in hordes.

Days were quiet. I was the only employee of the agency. Maybe the first? Something about it felt monumental. We worked in her spare room in her main house. I used her personal bathroom. I made lunch in her personal kitchen. I had full access to her home and I felt really awkward waltzing around in it. Most days we'd work in the spare room together, but some days she took meetings outside the makeshift office and left me in her house alone. I accepted her mail and packages and put them on the kitchen counter. She insisted that I help myself to everything in her kitchen cupboards if I got hungry. She treated me like a friend, not an employee. A friend that she was paying. But that wasn't why I stayed, even though I knew the work was not in line with my dreams of ad land. She had an enormous black and white border collie who greeted me every morning when I walked in the door. Every morning like clockwork, I'd unlock the door to the house and Fang would run up to me, get up on his hind legs and give me a massive bear hug with his huge, clumsy paws wrapped around my neck.

For someone who didn't grow up around dogs, this frightened me at first; I thought he was going to attack me. My boss saw the horror on my face and shouted at Fang to get down. But then he licked my face, and I learned that's how dogs show affection. Or he just liked the salty taste of my skin. I also later learned that dogs are God's gift to humans, even though we don't deserve them. They are the biggest serotonin boost. And that's why I enjoyed working there. Everyday I'd spend my lunch hour in the garden throwing an old, chewed up tennis ball to Fang and he'd run excitedly to bring it back to me all wet and slobbery. I ate my lunch, usually just a cheese sandwich from the garage shop, in the garden with Fang and he'd keep me company when I returned to my desk in the spare room. He was my favourite and only colleague for a long time and there was no one that my boss could hire who could ever be better than Fang, I thought.

My boss also had a cat but the cat was more wary of strangers. The cat didn't bother saying hello. The only time the cat would interact with me is when it wanted food, then the cat would slide its butt across my keyboard and give me this look. I can't remember the cat's name, and the only reason I can think of is that I'm a dog person. Fang brought out the dog person I never knew existed in me. For Christmas, I bought Fang and the cat gifts – the cat out of politeness, Fang because I loved him.

The weeks leading up to Christmas I barely did any work at

all. My boss was getting married soon and she had loads of wedding prep that still needed to be done, like printing invitations, cutting cards for name placements, organising wedding favours. I helped her with all of that. She would often pull me away from my desk into the kitchen and we'd sit around the breakfast nook, folding invitation cards. Matching wedding stationery. How stunning was that, I thought. This job was giving me work and life experience, because that's also where I learned how beautiful and classy weddings can actually be. In my culture, weddings were big and often disorganised; usually held in large industrial looking event rooms with plastic chairs and tables covered in throwaway white paper. The opposite of intimate and classy. The menu was a variation of the signature Coloured wedding dish: Cape Malay biryani and cold chicken, served with yellow rice and Appletizer. If you're lucky, the chicken would be garnished with cherry tomatoes and coriander leaves.

My boss's wedding was not like that. Her menu was an exquisite and thoughtful three course event, each dish complementing the one before it. It made me rethink the idea of weddings and everything that it could be. I wanted to remember all the tasteful touches from my boss's wedding so that I could integrate it into my own style, when MJ and I got married. But all the details cost money, and extravagant weddings seemed like a huge waste of money, if you didn't have any money.

A girl should know how to drive

~ 2007 ~

To get to Allura in Vredehoek every day, I took two taxis in the morning, and my dad fetched me in the afternoons when I finished work. Our relationship had improved over the years. We started speaking a little more, and I was able to get in the car with him without my mum being present. Between me starting college and graduating, he also bought himself a car, a white BMW motorsport, which he loved driving. He fetched me and my mum from work all the time. Until he got really sick and couldn't get in his car. The doctors said he had a stroke; a life-threatening condition that happens when the blood supply to part of the brain is cut off. Because of my dad's lone-wolf attitude, no one noticed his early symptoms. I also didn't realise how serious it was at the time. Most people need a long time to recover from a stroke and be able to do the things they used to do, and some people never fully recover. But my dad recovered miraculously. He regained his speech, he had no face distortion, and he was even able to drive the motorsport again. It was like he never even had a stroke. It made me happy hearing Issac Hayes' *Walk On By* from two roads away as my dad's car neared the house.

But the months before he was fully recovered, getting home from Vredehoek became difficult. My mum asked random people to give me a lift home. It wasn't a sustainable solution because every single day became a challenge. I could take a taxi to work in the mornings because it was safer to travel in the daylight. But I couldn't take the same taxi home from work in the evenings. The taxi route back was different, and I would need to wait for a taxi on a lonely street corner. The taxi would likely be empty after the last drop off, and therefore not ideal for a woman travelling solo, even in Vredehoek. I wasn't about to make that rookie mistake.

MJ and I were engaged at the time. He offered to fetch me from work everyday, while my dad was unable to drive. He lived in the neighbourhood close by Vredehoek and he'd be driving to Wynberg anyway when he came to see me. It made the most sense. But it also became a strain. MJ was spending a lot of time with me, and not his family. And I naively didn't think it would be a problem.

But I was an independent woman; I could make my own way. I came from a long line of fiercely independent women. My mum was vague about many things but one thing she drilled into my head was that women should be independent and not rely on anyone for anything. She was a strong feminist woman before feminism even became a thing. I decided to buy myself a car and learn how to drive. With the money I got from working at Allura, I could afford a deposit for a second-hand car and apply for car finance to cover the rest. I searched online for cheap, reliable, second-hand cars. I wondered how much SEO these websites were doing to improve their relevance.

Every time I showed interest in a car, my mum asked my dad to look at the specs and see if it was worth buying. Eventually I found *the one.* It was a white, 2l Renault Clio Sport; a two-door hatchback with tinted windows, a sunroof and full leather interior. It belonged to a model before me and she had a yellow rectangular sticker on the back window that read "Model in Transit". I pulled that off almost immediately because it didn't align with my punk ethos. The car stood parked and unused in our driveway for many months, because I still needed a driver's licence to drive it. I drove the car around the block a few times, but I lacked the confidence to drive any further than that.

I remember the first time my dad took me out on a driving lesson in that car. I was in my room, listening to Blink 182 and he came to the door and said,

"Let's go take a drive. You can drive around the block."

I just stared at him. What did he mean? Where was this coming from? Why did we need to take a drive right this second?

"The more you practise, the easier it will get," he continued.

He was right. And so I got up and followed him to the driveway where my car was parked. He got in the passenger side of the car and I got in the driver's seat.

"Can you pull the car out?" I asked. I was afraid I'd knock into the wall if I reversed into the street by myself.

I adjusted my seat, feeling the leather cool against my skin.

I glanced in all three mirrors, the way they teach you in the K53 method. And then I turned on the ignition, hearing the 2l engine purr.

"Right, remember that the bonnet needs to lift slightly, then you know that you have clutch control. Then you release the handbrake. Go for it," My dad said.

I followed his instructions to the T, the car moved forward slowly in first gear. I changed to second, gradually picking up pace to third, then fourth. We were cruising down Kent Road, passing all the neighbours, including aunty Nisa's house. I wasn't sure I could handle the power of this 2l turbo engine, so I stayed on fourth for a while. We neared the end of the block and my dad told me to take a left. I took a sharp left, underestimating the power steering and my dad yelled,

"Wait, slowly, too much, wait!"

But I lost control and crashed into the curb. It was more of a ding than a crash, and I was only doing 30 km/hour, but there was a loud bang. We both got out of the car and saw that I scraped my custom 15-inch rims against the pavement and burst the tyre. All the feelings I felt when I failed my driver's test twice before came crashing back in that moment and I sobbed. I wanted so desperately to be able to drive, but my brain wasn't connecting with my physical ability, or inability, to drive. My mind was already there, but my body needed to catch up. I wasn't ready. My dad tried to tell me that it was okay. I insisted that I didn't want to drive back home again, even though it was just two blocks away. I handed him the keys and reluctantly, he got out of the passenger side of the car and into the driver's seat.

"Everyone starts out this way, it's fine," he said as we drove the two blocks back home.

The tyre wasn't in a terrible condition, but it still needed to be replaced. It was a Saturday afternoon after 1pm in Cape Town. All the stores that were not part of a major shopping mall were already closed for the weekend. But my dad knew someone at a tyre fitment centre in Wynberg. He always knew someone somewhere who would drop everything to do him a favour.

I listened as he made the call, speaking to someone, asking them to keep the tyre centre open for a bit longer for his daughter. He dropped me off at home and then took my car to the tyre fitment centre. He returned shortly with a brand new tyre fitted perfectly around the rim that I scraped. I was grateful. He also called my mum to tell her what had happened and that I was upset. Looking back at this moment now, I don't understand why it felt so enormous and so emotional for me. Perhaps because it was a normal father-daughter moment, a father teaching his daughter how to drive and I ended it when I crashed into the pavement.

When Allura moved to Woodstock, it wasn't viable to take a taxi to work any more. The route to Woodstock wasn't safe. But I still didn't have my driver's licence and I still didn't know how to drive properly. My dad suggested that we use the mornings to get me more comfortable behind the wheel. So every morning I drove to Woodstock with my dad in the passenger seat of my car. When we'd get to my office, I'd get out of the car, he'd wait till I entered the building and then drive my car back home. That was the routine for a couple of months and it really did help me become more confident behind the wheel of my own car. I managed to avoid scraping any more expensive rims.

Driving to work in the mornings became our thing. I'd play my punk music boisterously and sometimes he'd sing along to the lyrics. Sometimes he'd tell my mum to tell me that I played the music way too loud. During those many mornings spent in the car, those 45 minutes in traffic from Wynberg to Woodstock, I got to know my dad a little better. It was the only time I would speak Afrikaans. As the first grandchild of ouma Dia's children, I grew up speaking Afrikaans. Everyone in our family home spoke Afrikaans to each other. And so naturally they spoke Afrikaans to me. As a child I learned how to speak Afrikaans first, then English. So technically, English is my second language, even though I studied it at school as a first language. And today, I claim it as my first language.

Afrikaans came with a whole lot of baggage. And I refused to speak it in front of my friends. There was this unspoken rule in the house that whenever I had friends over, no one should speak to me in Afrikaans. None of my friends spoke Afrikaans at home. To me, Afrikaans is another sign of your social status. Afrikaans, or rather, kombuis Afrikaans (informal Afrikaans) because that's what we really spoke at home, signified being poor. It signified growing up without the same privileges my peers did. It signified the old generation, the apartheid era. I didn't want MJ or any of my friends knowing that I spoke

Afrikaans because it was weird for someone my age to speak Afrikaans at home instead of English. The only person who still spoke to me in Afrikaans, was my dad.

Afrikaans was not my language, I decided. It was my heritage, but it was not my identity. I didn't want to speak the language that my ancestors were forced to speak when they were brought to the country as slaves.

We were going to make ads

~ 2008 ~

MJ and I got married in April of 2008. We had a big wedding with around 250 people at the reception. My mum made my wedding dress, the dress that kickstarted her second career in couture dressmaking. Ouma Dia was a dressmaker, a legacy skill that was passed down from Malay slaves. Dressmaking was a craft and a heritage. Malay slaves brought with them intricate sewing skills, embroidery techniques, and knowledge of textiles, all of which became a hidden yet enduring form of cultural expression. These skills were passed down quietly from generation to generation. Over time, what started as a skill honed under duress, as a means of income, evolved into a celebrated art, influencing fashion, community identity and family traditions.

My mum knew how to sew because she grew up watching ouma make beautiful gowns for all her customers. She didn't believe that she had it in her to make my wedding dress, but I believed she could. She also remembered every detail I told her about my boss at Allura's wedding and, with her sisters, brought the whole fairy tale to life for me. Matching wedding stationery, a three course menu that was also printed and placed on the tables, large cotton tablecloths that fell to the floor, chair covers with raw silk bows, tortured willow centre pieces, name place cards and wedding favours for all the guests were just a few memorable notes. It didn't look or feel like a typical Coloured wedding and not only because of the lack of biryani and cold chicken with yellow rice. We had reshaped the idea of what a wedding could be. It had the bones and character of a White wedding, in the heart of Constantia — a previously declared White neighbourhood. Our friends and family were surprised, but I like to think pleasantly surprised. I do wonder why it was important for us to have these things at my wedding, to make such a statement when everyone who got married that year wasn't really phased about those details. Memories of "sy will soos die wittes wees" (she wants to be White) kept echoing in my head.

Before the wedding, I resigned from Allura and left Fang and the cat. I didn't see my career progressing in SEO, and I didn't want to lose sight of the ad land dream. I accepted an offer at a boutique digital agency as Junior Operations Executive. Let's call them Advertise.ly. My dad and I took a new route to work in the mornings. He showed me how to drive to the Foreshore to get to my new office.

"Okay, good luck for your first day and enjoy it. This is going to be a good one," he said as he dropped me off in front of the face brick building.

"Okay," I said absently as I grabbed my bag from the back seat and headed inside.

I'd only been to their office twice before for my interviews, so I still felt a tinge of nerves while entering the office on my own. As I exited the elevators on the top floor, I thought, this is it. This is advertising. Finally, I was where I wanted to be. *Or so she thought,* the narrator said.

The brightly-lit open-plan office at Advertise.ly was filled with white-washed desks set up in hubs of four. There was a background hum of cheerful office banter. The wraparound windows boasted the view of Cape Town CBD (Central Business District), majestic as always. Bill, the owner and CEO, welcomed me and introduced me to the rest of the team. He showed me where I would sit and then gave me a tour of the office. I couldn't stop smiling as I took it all in. I didn't know what I would be working on exactly, but I knew that it would be some form of advertising. That's what Bill told me in the interview. I knew that this is where I would be making ads. This was the place. I made it, I thought.

On my second day I didn't have any real work assignments, so I decided to assign some to myself. Coming from an SEO firm, I decided to focus on what I knew. I created an SEO strategy for Advertise.ly's own brand. I pitched the idea to my manager, told him about the benefits of doing this and the output he could expect from me in a couple of days. Basically, everything I learned from my previous boss at Allura, where I left Fang. He was satisfied with that approach, and so I continued on with doing my own thing. Autonomy. My ideal performance state. I stayed in my corner, quietly creating something that no one in the business had ever done before.

One morning my manager told me, "You're the most senior SEO in the business, but you're so young."

I smiled, not knowing what to make of this statement. It was a statement, not a compliment. It was only then I really started paying attention to the physical appearances of the people around me. Yes, I was the youngest. It was also then when I first noticed that I was also the tannest person in the office. Everyone around me at Advertise.ly was White. This didn't matter to me. I was used to being the only person of colour in the room, so much so, that I forgot to notice. But I did question whether other people noticed, and what they saw when they looked at me.

My title was Junior Operations Executive but I wasn't quite sure what was expected of me. Bill said that they liked my CV and what I could bring to the business. But several weeks into my role, I still didn't have any job specifications or career expectations laid out. I completed my SEO strategy but that didn't go anywhere because the business didn't have any resources to implement my strategy. We had no development team who could make the technical code or content changes. We didn't have a CMS. And honestly, I don't think that SEO was a business goal at the time. Not for clients, and not for Advertise.ly's own brand. Was my two weeks spent on this strategy wasted? Well, maybe.

Weeks went by when I did more of the same. Admin and ad hoc tasks. What am I doing here? Why did they hire me? What am I supposed to do? I kept asking myself. I didn't question why there weren't more people like me, Coloureds, working here. I had already gotten used to and accepted that people of colour don't often end up in the advertising and creative industry. This made me very cautious of rocking the boat. I wanted to tread lightly; if I just kept my head down and did as I was told, I'd fit in and things would be okay.

More weeks went by with an unwritten job spec and no goals. I helped out the ad trafficking team, as that part of the business was bursting at the seams and they were understaffed. I learnt the ropes quickly and in no time I was able to traffic an ad campaign to servers across the globe. Advertise.ly was part of a global ad server tech network that allowed publishers to create, distribute, optimise and measure their digital ad campaigns across any and all screens. We were essentially in control of the digital displays of several blue chip brands in the country. On paper, this seemed like the ideal place for an aspiring ad copywriter to be. The only thing missing here was that we didn't make ads.

Ad creative would land in our inboxes, already conceptualised and polished by the publishers and brands' in-house creative team, and it was our job to assess the quality of the creative. That meant that I spent most of my days checking if the buttons on a banner worked, did what it said it does, sense-checking the content and then loading it onto our ad systems to get it published into the world. It was called ad trafficking and it bored me to death. Deep inside, I knew that this was against the grain of what I wanted to do when I grew up. It was not what I wanted to do when I set out to study copywriting. One would argue that it was, in fact, advertising, but it wasn't the glorious, advertising world that I was chasing.

I knew I had to leave Advertise.ly. But I couldn't move just yet because it was a job that paid money, and I needed that. I didn't have another job lined up, so if I really wanted to leave this job, I'd better get another job lined up. But it took an age for me to get my first job, and then another couple of months to get this job, and neither were exactly what I wanted to do in life. Was I being too picky? Did I need to scale down my needs and focus on the objective at hand: earning money? It felt like the same cycle that people of colour are used to year in and year out. Pack your interests and passions away and focus on working hard and earning money. This was the life we were used to, but it was not the life I wanted to build for myself. I wanted something different. I wanted something more.

Janazah prayers and rejection letters

In the winter of 2008 I lost my dad. *I didn't lose him*. I hate that we use that word when people you love die. *The public hospital we trusted him with* lost him.

After MJ and I got married, my dad stopped driving me to work and I started spending less and less time with him. We stopped our morning routines to work because MJ drove me to work. I'd still do family nights at our family home every Friday eve, but my dad wouldn't always be there. I hardly saw him after I got married. One Friday night when I didn't go to family night, my dad fell ill. My mum and her sisters rushed my dad to hospital but no one bothered to tell me. So while I sat in my blissful ignorance, watching *Supernatural* in our 3rd floor apartment around the corner from my parents' house, my dad was being rushed to the emergency ward of the public hospital.

I don't remember when the news eventually came to me. I don't remember who told me, or what they told me. I just remember standing in the filthy hallway of Victoria Hospital in Wynberg the next day, the off-yellow paint on the walls glaring at me. The doors to one of the wards swung open as a doctor went inside and I caught a glimpse of my dad on a hospital bed. He was sitting upright. He wore those ridiculous hospital robes and he had what looked like a million tubes attached to his body. His face just didn't look right.

I tried to catch his eye without saying anything, in my quiet way, in our non-verbal way of communicating. He didn't see me. I tried to peep through the tiny glass square in the door, but I couldn't make out what was happening. Then, moments later, we were outside. I watched as the world exploded around me. Paramedics were wheeling my dad out to an ambulance with its siren already on and ready to go. In the midst of the chaos I made out that we were headed to Groote Schuur Hospital. The ambulance. Were taking. My dad. To Groote Schuur Hospital. No one in my family has ever returned home alive from Groote Schuur hospital. And that's when I knew it was serious.

Medics were shouting orders, opening ambulance doors. In the background I could hear my mum asking questions to which no one replied. I watched my dad lay with his eyes closed on the stretcher and all the tubes still attached to his body. That's when MJ pulled me close and I felt my face was wet. Tears. I was crying.

We spent hours and hours at Groote Schuur Hospital. Day turned into night and we sat in the waiting room waiting for an update. My dad had a stroke. He'd had a stroke before and recovered from it, and even continued to drive. He'll be fine, I thought. He always is. Two women in contrasting pale and dark blue uniforms asked if I wanted to see him. I said no, I don't want to. I'll just wait here till they've done their things and we can take him home. But we never did get to take him home. Not alive anyway.

Inside the waiting room, the faded beige paint was peeling from the walls. I read all the words on all the posters while the cold of the plastic chairs rippled through my body. Different families passed through the room throughout the night. Finally, a doctor came out and said they had some news. They led us to a private room. As we walked there through the chaos in the long hallway of general admissions, my mum started sobbing.

We eventually entered the private room, which was just someone's cluttered office space. The room was small and it suffocated me. We sat around a table that looked like it belonged in a school cafeteria. There were files everywhere, an old box-shaped computer on a desk and three plastic chairs.

"Mrs Adams, I'm afraid he didn't make it," the doctor said.

I was in the room but I wasn't really in the room. It was like my brain had decided to remove itself from my body right there and then. Even though it's been years and I was out of practice, my body still remembered how to zombify itself again. Everything after "he didn't make it," sounded like the adults speaking in the Charlie Brown cartoons. Wah wah wah wah.

We left the room and I went to see my dad then. I stood behind the curtain in a public ward, given as much privacy as that plastic curtain provided. The noise and chaos outside the curtain blended with everything that was happening inside my head that very moment. Sirens were going off, tables were falling, wheels were being pushed and the inner walls of my brain started to collapse. My head felt thick and my breath short. I felt my rib cage tighten, trying to suffocate me. I felt my heartbeat in my throat as I stared at the dead body in front of me, that was my dad. I think MJ was next to me, watching as I shoved my dad. Tugging at him, daring him to move, demanding him to breathe, whispering at him to wake up.

I watched his lifeless body bounce side to side as I kept shoving him, willing him to come back. It wasn't his turn yet. I needed more time with him. I needed him to know that.

"Wake up!" I insisted.

Everything after that moment was a blur to me. I don't remember getting home from the hospital. I remember MJ calling my manager to let him know, but after that I have no recollection. We'd seen a lot of deaths in the family before so I knew from those experiences that my mum probably had a lot of things to organise. I couldn't imagine how to make the call to your family and friends, telling them that your husband had just died, but my mum must have done it, because we had the [10]janazah the next day.

* * *

I woke up to the soothing sounds of melodic prayer gently

---

[10] An Arabic term used in Cape Town to refer to a funeral or burial.

fluttering through the air. It was peaceful. I knew that the peace would only extend to the end of my childhood bedroom, and outside was a different story. We must have spent the night there, or arrived there very early, and I fell asleep. I can't remember. I opened the door of my old bedroom and instantly felt the chaos. Walking through the house on my socks, I tried to find my mum through the sea of people who were stepping in and out of our home, in our rooms, trying to lend a helping hand for the funeral. My dad knew everyone, and everyone who knew him wanted to be there to pay their respects. I passed my parents' bedroom, where the prayer was coming from. My dad's body was placed on an elevated bed in the centre of the room. The walls were lined with seats filled by people who may or may not have known my dad, praying for him, reading from the Quran. The room was completely rearranged for this purpose. He was surrounded by prayer, and I loved that for him. I didn't go into the room. I never saw his face again since that night in the hospital, when he didn't see me, when it was too late.

I continued through the house, still trying to find my mum or MJ. Women and men that I didn't recognise came up to me and hugged me while whispering in my ear, saying sorry for my loss. Their tear-stained cheeks created a sticky mess in my neck as they hugged me. I wiped it away almost immediately, but it still left me feeling grosse. I wanted to be alone, but as soon as I left my room it was also transformed to a seating area for mourners. I had nowhere to really be alone.

My mum found me wandering through the house.

"Can you put a scarf on?" she instructed.

I continued to wander in melancholy. Someone wrapped a scarf around my head. I think, one of my aunties. My mind was racing with thoughts I couldn't process. What was he thinking in those final moments before death? How was he feeling? Was he comfortable? Was he in pain? Did he know he was about to die? Was there something he wanted to do before he died? Was he happy? Did he think about me? Did he know I loved him? Was he still alive on that bed in the room? Someone better check his breathing before they lower him into the ground and bury him alive. What if he is buried alive and he can't get back out from underground? How can we know for sure that he really was dead? Will someone double check this? I thought of my dad suffocating underneath the earth.

Our home was filling up even more with people I'd never seen before, but who somehow knew me. Maybe I knew them but couldn't recognise them as all I could see for faces was a blurry pile of features. Large steel pots of biryani were on the cooker, supervised by aunties; the aromatic smell of the biryani sent my stomach grumbling. It was almost time. The final prayer would be said, and the last chance to see my dad, before his body would be carried out of the house and into the cemetery.

Another blurry face walked up towards me, handed me a permanent marker and a thick wooden plank; a temporary burial marker for my dad's grave.

"What do you want me to write?" I asked.

"Just his name and surname, year of birth to this year and 786 (In the name of God)," they said.

I lay down on the floor of my childhood bedroom, crouched over my dad's burial marker, etching his name into the wood. Each letter took longer than usual to write as tears clouded my vision. I was conscious of the many eyes watching me and I didn't care. In that moment, nothing felt real. The only reality that I seemed to grasp was that this is when we say goodbye to my dad and bury him underground. I think that was the exact moment when something inside me broke forever.

* * *

The summer came and brought along with it a new sense of nostalgia. Instead of Isaac Hayes' *Walk On By* playing loudly from my dad's white BMW motorsport, the streets were silent. I resumed my natural state of dealing with trauma and floated like a zombie through the world. Not experiencing, just existing. I later learned in therapy that this coping mechanism often stems from trauma or stress. The emotional numbness or blunting can manifest as feeling flat, disconnected from others and oneself, or lacking the ability to express emotions. It's about not feeling safe to express emotions, so the opposite occurs, suppressing. This coping strategy usually provides short-term comfort and protection from intense emotional distress, but it can hinder emotional healing and lead to prolonged feelings of detachment. The cause is not identified as to why people develop this sort of numbing, but it usually presents in patients with a high level of stress that causes the brain to slip into survival mode.

Losing my dad made me realise that life was extremely short and made me evaluate all the other things in my life that weren't working. Like, working in a job that didn't energise me. I was still chasing my dream of wanting to make ads. I wanted to see my work on TV, on billboards, in magazines around the city. And right now, I wasn't doing that.

I loved working at Advertise.ly. Not for the work, but for the people. I met good people there, the best kind of people, some of whom I'm still friends with today. We shared a love of punk rock music, we spent weekends together, we sang along to rock concerts in the sunset at Kirstenbosch Gardens. We became really good friends. My manager was one of the first people MJ called when we were at the hospital to tell him the news of my dad passing. They gave me unlimited time off work without any questions, sent me flowers to our home and after a week and a bit when I eventually felt strong enough to go back to work, everyone checked in on me to make sure I was okay. And through my friends at Advertise.ly, I met people from one of our biggest publishers: a digital marketing agency that we'll call Indigo Star.

Take everything you know from my, and possibly your, experience of searching for a job in a dying economy, in an industry where you're not designed to be in, and add to it a third factor: trying to hide the grief of losing your father. It took all of my energy that season to try and show up and be my best self in interviews. I still kept on to the hope of finding my dream job. I wanted to make ads. I wanted to see my words across a billboard by the sea. I wanted to be *ad famous*. And I wasn't going to get that by trafficking someone else's creative concepts.

Every night I came home and cried myself to sleep after supper. Partly for the time with my dad I would never get back and partly because I felt like I was never going to land my big break. My mum had sacrificed all she had for me to study copywriting so that I could make it big in advertising. So this couldn't be it for me. Could it? There had to be something more out there for me. Something's gotta give. I channelled my pain into applying for jobs. The right jobs. The ones where I would be in the driver's seat of creating beautiful, emotive ads. I applied to small agencies, big agencies, medium-sized agencies, in-house brand creative teams. But no one wanted an inexperienced copywriter who didn't even go to proper Ad School.

We regret to inform you that the position you've applied for has already been filled.

We decided to go with someone who was a better fit for us culturally.

We've reviewed this end and unfortunately we just don't think you'd be quite right for this role.

And so it went, on and on for months.

Without any traditional ad agency experience and no Ad School background, it was proving harder to get to my dream job than

I thought. The goal kept moving further and further away.

"We're hiring for an in-house copywriter, why don't you apply?" One of the girls from the publisher agency, Indigo Star, told me.

It wasn't exactly ad copywriting. It was more of the same thing I did at Allura with Fang, the border collie. But at least it was copywriting and that was closer to the field I studied than trafficking ad campaigns.

"Yeah okay, I'll go for it."

The rise of social media

~ 2009 ~

One interview, two interviews and a meet-and-greet with the CEO and somehow they decided that I was a good fit for the role of SEO Copywriter. I joined a small team of SEO Copywriters at Indigo Star who worked hand in hand with the SEO Strategists, so, splitting up the strategy and content work that I did all on my own at Allura. Here I could focus solely on writing.

The company was very diverse. I wasn't the only person of colour at the agency and that made me settle into the team immediately. The culture was great. My team was great. I was still plugging keywords into 500-word articles but only now, I was doing it for well-known brands and I got paid a whole lot more. For a long time, work was good. My manager was great. I even forgot about making ads for a while. I was content. And I was making content. Apart from losing my dad, life was good.

The agency was doing so well that we hired another copywriter. She was lovely and we took turns editing each other's work. And then one day she asked me to print something for her because her computer wasn't connected to the printer yet. It was her payslip. She wanted me to print her payslip. I probably shouldn't have looked, but when I realised that it was too late. We had the same job title. We had the same level of experience, according to LinkedIn. (Of course I was going to check). We performed the same role day in and day out, editing each other's work. But her salary was three times more than mine, and that didn't make any sense. Until it dawned on me and then it made perfect sense. She was White, and I was Coloured.

As a woman I respected her for not keeping her salary a secret from me. She probably thought I was earning the same. My issue was not with her, it was with the system that classed us in different pay brackets because of the colour of our skin, probably. And secondly, with the person who hired us around the same time, offering me less than what my White colleague was offered. After I discovered that, it made working for the agency really hard. I lost interest in the work and lost faith in the leaders of the business. I could've been one of those people who quietly quit. Quiet quitting by definition means to remain in one's workplace while not actively going above and beyond. The term itself wasn't coined until after the 2020 pandemic, when people had more time to reflect, reassess their priorities and the state of humanity, but people were quietly quitting long before then. I couldn't do it. It just wasn't in my DNA. So I did what any idiot would do in my position. I tried to find a way to make the business generate more money, instead of advocating for more money for myself.

It was 2009 and social media was in its infancy. Companies

certainly weren't thinking about social media strategy as a business offering. But I was. My head was spinning with all sorts of ideas for brand campaigns on social media. But I didn't have any real brands to test with. So I decided to test on our own brand, Indigo Star. In a few short weeks, Indigo Star was creating hype on Facebook and Twitter. I decided to focus on those two social media channels as a start. Facebook to show the company culture and Twitter for business insights and industry news. It was my fun side project when I managed to hit my word count deadline early, still working as an SEO Copywriter.

"We should pitch social media," I said to the Managing Director of Indigo Star.

"What do you mean?" he asked.

"Social media as a service. Another marketing channel for brands," I continued.

We were working on a pitch for a new client, a big one. I offered to work on a few ideas for launching the brand on social media that we could present in the pitch meeting.

"Send me some examples by the end of the day and we'll see," said MD.
   And so I did.

And that's how the Social Media Marketing department at Indigo Star was born. My job title was now split into Copywriter/Social Media Strategist. I spent 50% of my time plugging keywords into 500-word articles published somewhere in the depths of the internet. And the other 50% of my time I dreamed up magical social media brand campaigns.

On our way back from a client meeting, the MD said to me, "You're really good at this, Leilah and clients love you. Keep doing what you're doing."

My manager, the head of content, loved that the copywriting department was also now being recognised as the social media department. He got credit for it no doubt. He said we should grow the department so that we had a whole team of social media specialists and copywriters in one department. Yeah that sounded great, I thought. Followed by the immediate thought of, "wait a minute - this whole idea was mine!" Social media as an additional product offering was my idea. Pitching our first social media client was my idea. Developing that first pitch was all me, no supervision from my manager. Building out the content plans, the processes, the templates, the strategies were all my work. I did this. All by myself. So what if *I* grew this department? What if *I* built out this department with a team of specialists? What if *I* led this new fictional team?

I pitched the idea to my MD, and he said if I could win two more pitches for social media then I had the budget to fund this department. I didn't stop to calculate if that included a pay rise for myself. I was too busy exploring this new marketing channel and all its possibilities. Ad land could wait, I was having fun on social media for now.

* * *

The next few months I focused all of my energy into new business pitches.

"What brands are you targeting?" I asked the new business director

"This one and this one, but they don't want social."

"Get me in the room," I insisted.

I pitched to anyone who would listen, even though pitching wasn't really my super power. In my quiet, soft-spoken way, I won clients over to see social media as a service. I grew the department, until we had too much work for just one person to do. And so I got approval to hire the second employee of the newly developed social media department. My little department doubled in size and we were charging brands for products that I had literally made up: Social Media Strategy, Community Management, Concept Development, Campaign Planning, Content Creation, Social Listening and Reporting.

I stopped introducing myself as the part time social media strategist and introduced myself as the head of social media. Boom. It was an instant lift on my CV. My salary, on the other hand, remained the same. Three times less than what a White copywriter was making at the same company. Is that partly my fault, for not advocating for a pay rise after all this time? I asked myself. Well, probably. You know the saying: if you don't ask, you'll never get. And I didn't ask.

I wasn't raised to ask for money. In my culture it was awkward to talk about money in the workplace. Especially in a workplace where just a few years ago people of colour were not seen. So we adopt an attitude of we take what we can get and we have to be really grateful for every opportunity. Opportunities that were not available to our parents and grandparents before us. To me that translated to a prestigious job title in a digital marketing agency owned by a White man. I was so grateful. And of course I wasn't going to ask for a pay rise.

As an early adopter of social for business, I got invited to social media tech talks, webinars, workshops hosted by other agencies and product businesses. I met more people, expanded my network and got free training to level up my skills. It was those years where I honed my craft and started to think about what best in class looks like, my north star.

The first person I hired for my team was another copywriter. My point of view was that social is all about content. If you wanted to make your brand social stand out, you needed a content specialist who knew how to create and activate an engaging content strategy. Those years on Facebook, you'd see a lot of brands publishing content to their Pages without even checking if the grammar was correct. That translated to many blue chip brands coming across as unprofessional online. There was a phase when several brands were caught online in a social media blunder. I knew the way to fix it was a content quality system. A significant number of industry folks still believed that social media was a passing fad and should be given to the intern, the IT department or the web administrators to manage. But this is your brand! Would you give your TV commercial to just about anyone to film? Of course not, so why treat social media any differently? A good content strategy was the basis of every successful social media campaign. You need imagination, creativity, empathy to think like a user and superb communication skills in order to be the public voice of the brand. That approach is sort of the norm now, but it wasn't always that way.

I had a plan when I hired the first social media copywriter in my team. I wanted us to create jaw-dropping social media campaigns that were going to be next year's strategists' case studies for the future. I wanted us to be the best in class. I wanted us to set the tone for the industry. I was never planning on being a manager that was no longer connected to the work. My management style was to lead by example; be so good at the craft that I inspired my team with my passion. I knew that to get the team where I wanted it to be, we needed to be brave, take risks, lean into our creativity the way that technical SEO copywriting didn't require.

Be sure not to burn out before you are fully lit

~ 2012 ~

More and more brands were starting to launch on social media, which meant more agencies had started to adopt social media as a serious product offering. Someone once told me that the easiest way to get a pay rise was to change jobs. So I thought, I could stay and grow this little department, or I could take my skills and move to a bigger agency. I still wasn't prepared to ask for a pay rise, but I did believe that I was worth more than what I was getting paid. I also wanted to be at a company with a bigger budget, more investment in social media and more room for me to grow.

So I started interviewing again. But this time, I had a newfound confidence in my back pocket. The world was pivoting to digital and I had already figured out how to make branding and marketing relevant on a new, growing marketing channel: social media. I guess my lecturer was right all along about digital being the future.

The dream of making billboards along the coast at a traditional ad agency was fading. Did I still want it? I don't know. The prospect of being a leader in the social space, when it was still in its infancy in the country, was massive. And so I honed in on that. I believed that this was the next chapter. I stopped pushing so hard to get noticed by the Ogilvies, the Saatchies, the J Walter Thompsons. Sure, I wanted to make ads, but now I knew that they should be on social media and not on billboards.

I targeted companies who had some digital investment in their business already, so that when I pitched myself as a social media specialist, it wouldn't be a complete hard sell. I applied for a number of roles that all had some degree of social media management included:

- Online Marketing Manager
- Social Media Manager
- Communications Manager
- Head of Editorial
- Community Manager
- Social Media Strategist
- Online Copywriter
- Senior Content Lead
- Social Media Administrator
- Online Content Manager
- Content Writer

Every interview was a learning experience, never a waste. I learnt a great deal about the state of the social media industry in South Africa, specifically, how young the industry was. One digital creative agency I applied at, a pedigree agency, told me that they didn't see content strategy as part of their social media offering, that I maybe needed to rethink how I position myself when I go to my next interview. They packaged it as some *friendly advice*. To them, social media for brands was managed by their account directors. No strategy, just community management. Hah.

I went to so many interviews at so many different companies. Some companies knew about social for business, some thought they knew and some had no idea at all.

Applying for jobs became a professional sport for me. Every night after work I would start writing cover letters and emailing my CV into the ether. I wasn't getting anywhere with this approach, not even a reply to say that the position had been filled. So I tried a different tactic. For as long as I'd wanted to make ads, I'd wanted to win awards for my ads. I wanted to win a Gold Cannes Lion. The ad industry had many award organisations such as the Loeries, the Bookmarks, the D&AD Pencils, the Webbys, the Shorties and the Clio awards, but The Cannes Lion award is the most prestigious.

My new tactic to find a job was to wait for the announcement of these awards, to see the winners and the agencies who were making the kind of work that I wanted to make. I then reached out to these agencies' creative directors on LinkedIn. At first it was casual, just to connect and introduce myself. And then I started sending out speculative job applications to the same agencies. I looked at their case studies to see which brands were on their books. I created my own concepts for campaigns for their clients, based on fake briefs I created for myself, and I sent these along with my job applications.

I didn't go to Ad School, so I didn't have a portfolio. With no Ad School, I didn't get the support with an internship at a real ad agency. And this led to the number one deal-breaker: no ad agency experience. I was a journalism graduate who wanted to break into the ad world. And I had nothing to show and no one to vouch for me. No mentor to show me the ropes, to inspire me. There was no one I knew who worked in ad land, especially no one I knew who looked like me. This was my way of building up my portfolio, making it on my own.

And it worked. Along with the newfound confidence, I started to make headway with the job hunt. I interviewed at an online gaming company; a small, testbed company born from one of the big tech companies today that make computers. You're probably using one of their computers right now. The testbed made a series of digital mobile games. The games had a strong audience but they wanted to reach more people and create a hype around the games. They wanted to create this hype on social media where they believed their potential audience was. And they wanted me to do it for them. Their offer was almost double my salary at Indigo Star.

I also interviewed at one of my dream digital agencies. They were big, established and had evolved from a traditional ad agency to a full-scale digital operation. They were already doing social media and had a roster of clients for me to work with. They were looking for a head of social and offered me the job. I had never before been in the position where *I* could choose between the jobs I wanted. I was usually on the other side of the tough choice, and if I was lucky, the company would choose me above another candidate. Person. Now here I was, with a choice of two great job offers. I revelled in the luxury of having a choice.

The mobile gaming company was not on my plan, but it would mean I could focus wholeheartedly on the social media strategy element of the job - the part I loved most. And it was big tech. The head of social role would no doubt come with the prestige I've been chasing all these years - leading a well-known creative agency into the digital era. I could see the awards in my future. And I could finally call myself a thoroughbred creative, also something I've always wanted. But being the head of a department meant I would be responsible for all the other filler tasks that came with managing a whole department: pitching, processes, people management, budgets, forecasts, reporting and all of the boring admin stuff that didn't energise me. It would mean I would spend less time making cool social media campaigns and more time making sure the department was operationally sound. It would mean less time making ads, my true passion.

With a heavy heart, I said no to the dream agency. I accepted the offer at the online gaming company. The dream agency counter-offered, called and begged me to sign with them, but I chose the gaming company, again. It only took me three weeks to realise that it was the absolute wrong choice. But by then it was too late. I tried to go back to the dream agency, tell them I've made a mistake. But by then they changed their mind too. They said that on second thought they didn't think I was senior enough for the role after all and had already hired someone else. I was shattered.

What was I thinking taking this job? I had no business promoting a game that I didn't know how to play anyway. I was not in tune with audience needs, I didn't understand why the game mattered and I didn't believe any of the reasons I was told that the game would be popular. With everything else on the app stores at the time, I felt the game lacked basic features and enhancements that other games had. And those games were already in the top 10 list of most downloaded apps in the app stores. We didn't have the budget or the time to make those enhancements, but they wanted a big marketing push. Without investment in those areas, I couldn't really do my job properly: promoting a game to an audience who expected better. Marketing should be the final step in your product design lifecycle. It shouldn't be used as a Band Aid to hide all the holes in the product.

"Quit your job if you're so unhappy," MJ told me.

"I have a car to pay, my credit card and we have bills." I managed through tears of frustration.

"I'll pay for it," he continued.

"How will it look on my CV? Three weeks at a job?"

"Just remove it from your CV. You will find another job soon. You have experience now, and you're really good at what you do. Just quit."

And so with the support of my husband, I quit my job without having another job lined up first. MJ gave me permission to choose happiness first, to take a break, to rest and recharge. After all the energy it took to put myself back together when my dad died, I was burnt out. I didn't think anyone noticed, but MJ did.

Being unemployed was difficult for me. It felt unnatural at best. I immediately reached out to the people I didn't reply to when the two offers rolled in the previous month. Were they still looking to fill the role? I asked. Had they found someone yet? I asked hopefully. Yes, yes they had. It was a fast-moving industry and I was about four weeks too late. After two-ish months of being unemployed I decided to apply for just any role again. I needed to work. I decided I'd take any other interesting job. For the experience. For the money. I even considered calling up Bojan at the tattoo shop. But I'd at least wait a week to see if any of the emails landed.

Becoming best in class

~ 2013 ~

I don't remember what I was doing when the email arrived in my inbox that day. The number in my email tab went from (0) to (1) and I instantly switched to the tab to open the email with the subject line: Social Media Administrator.

```
Hi Leilah,

I got your contact details and CV from a colleague
of mine. We are presently looking for a social media
administrator within our growing social media
department.

The role includes a number of responsibilities from
social platform management, strategic work,
copywriting, analytics to mention but a few.

If you would be interested to join me for a meeting
to discuss the position please drop me a mail or
give me a call as soon as you can.

All the best,
```

From Head of Social at my dream agency to Social Media Administrator at Iridium - an agency I'd never heard of before. Days went by where I wallowed in regret. It was all-consuming and I blamed myself for missing the opportunity of my dreams. Everyone only gets one big break. My big break, the one I'd been chasing my entire career, had come and I had passed it up to try and make it in a gaming company. I don't even like games. I almost didn't reply to that email. Social Media Administrator? Pfff. Surely that's a junior role. I was overqualified for it. I was too good for that.

And while I turned my nose up at the prospect of this job, I also thought, well, beggars can't be choosers. And so I responded to the email. Little did I know that this would be the email that changed the course of my life forever.

When they told me that they needed someone to join their growing social media department, they weren't joking. It really was fledgling. This department had no structure or processes in place, no value proposition, no pitch materials, nothing. Luckily for them, I knew exactly how to fix all of that. It was a challenge that I welcomed with open arms.

For the most part I was left to my own devices. Autonomous. My ideal performance state, I remembered. My manager quickly saw my strengths and gave me the autonomy I needed in order to do my best work. And so I worked on improving our SLAs (Service Level Agreements) and developing a product strategy, shaping the agency's social product offering, from strategy to activation, community management, concept development, campaign planning, content creation, voice and tone work, event coverage, as well as measurement and reporting. I did all of this alongside delivering important work we had already committed to for a big automobile brand. The one with the three pointed star.

It didn't take me long to get to know the business problems, client problems and the areas of opportunity to show real value. Within a month they changed my title from social media administrator to social media analyst which gave me a bit more seniority. Not much, but more than an administrator. I was already owning the responsibility, and I guess the title change was their way of acknowledging my efforts.

I got feedback from account directors that whenever they were in meetings with clients, they'd ask who the person was managing their social media account. They were really happy that I was working on their social content strategy and that made me feel warm inside. I kept pushing to do more, be better, deliver more value. At the time social media was all about likes. And I grew their Facebook page from 10 000 likes to over 3 million in a few short weeks. Likes turned into brand advocates who were in love with the brand we were building.

"How did you do it?" people would often ask me.

It's just a content strategy. Define your content pillars, what you want to say and when you want to say it, create jaw-droppingly great visual content (it was easy with a sexy automobile brand) and post consistently.

Within the timeline of hiring me to me passing my probation, we'd gone from a growing social media department to a well-oiled machine. All my manager had to do was focus on new business development. That, and taking the credit for my work apparently.

I'm in the business of boosting revenue

I started getting invites to meetings with the department leads, because people started noticing my work and they wanted to hear my ideas. By then, I had also mastered the art of shouting about my work on email: the introvert's tool for self-promotion. And as an introverted person of colour, you need to work extra hard at self-promotion to get noticed.

My manager enjoyed the great work that I did, but only if he could get all the merit for it. As soon as people started singling me out, praising me, it became a problem. He started cutting me out of meetings and undermining me. And to this day, I still wonder if I was overreacting.

There was a meeting that was about to start. It was five minutes before kickoff. Like everyone else invited to the meeting, I took my company branded notebook and made my way to the glass-partitioned box in the corner of the office. All the senior specialists and heads of departments entered the room, including my manager, with me following close behind. And as I was about to enter the room, my manager shut the glass door behind him, giving me a smile as the door closed in my face.

I opened the door and he turned towards me, "Oh, did you need something from me?"

"No, I'm in this meeting too," I mumbled.

"Oh well, I can update you. We probably don't need both of us in the same meeting," He said while nodding towards the door for me to leave.

What was this patriarchy? Was he actually nodding towards the door for me to leave the room? What year was I in? I was prepared to let that incident go, but then a version of it happened again.

It was the start of another meeting, a different day, a different time. As I entered the meeting room, my manager collected the dirty plates and cake wrappers left behind on the table from a previous meeting. He placed the tray in my hands and with a swooshing movement of his hand, he said,

"Off you go, shoo."

So with the tray already in my hands, I did as I was told and walked away.

In another meeting he asked me to make him a cup of tea and bring it to him in the meeting. Was I his assistant? Was it because I was female or because I was Coloured? This was the question I kept asking myself when these weird incidents happened. And they happened often. Why was he deliberately trying to cut me out of meetings where I was clearly involved in the project? Why was no one saying anything when they witnessed it? Was it so normalised in the culture that the brown woman should be serving tea to the White man? What was going on here?

***

Months went by with my manager treating me like his assistant. Maybe I was his assistant, and I was just overachieving at work? It confused me why he treated me like the help. It was also embarrassing, and it hurt.

One evening after work, I sat in my blue Renault Clio S with the racing stripes in the dimly lit parking area of the Upper East Side Hotel in Woodstock — where our offices were located. When my dad passed away, I finally went and got my driver's licence. I drove the old white Clio with the sunroof for a few epic years with confidence, and without my dad there for moral support. I loved that car so much. But it became too expensive to maintain in the end. The 2L engine started packing up, the ABS brakes needed replacing every few months, the wiring for the electric windows stopped working. Pick anything that could go wrong in that car, and it did. I sold it and used the little money I got back for it as a deposit for the newer Clio. The one I was sitting crying in now. My dad would have loved the car.

I put my key in the ignition and all the frustration of the day exploded from inside of me. Here I was, again, crying about work in the dark. I felt hopeless. Nothing has changed since apartheid and nothing was going to change. There was no concrete evidence or anything tangible I could point to, to explain why I felt the way I did. And no one can change things for you just based on feelings.

Things had gotten worse between my manager and I. He continued with the micro-aggressions and I continuously brushed it off, as it continued to chip away at my self-worth. And then he hired his friend and appointed her social media strategist. The plan was for me to hand over all the work that I was doing to her, as she came in as more senior. I didn't know where that left me and I wasn't ready to find out. But also, I had no moves to play.

People were leaving the office and walking through the parking lot. I had to move but I was a complete wreck. Through my blackout tinted windows, Katy from media planning spotted me sobbing in the car. She climbed inside the passenger seat and that was the first time I told anyone what I had been experiencing the past few months working with my manager. That night, I got the first decent night's sleep in a long time.

We had supper next door at my mum's as usual. She made chicken biryani with soft, jasmine-style rice, the way MJ likes it. My mum grew up in a time where women served the men of the household their food, out of respect as they were the breadwinners. Even though it was a different time, and I kept reminding her of gender equality, she still enjoyed doing that and cooking MJ's favourite food as the only man in the household - with my dad passed on.

After supper my mum would listen attentively to how my day

went. I wouldn't leave out any detail and I'd watch as she and MJ got angry and annoyed as they relived the injustices of my day through my words. When the sun set, MJ and I would go home next door and retire in front of the TV for the evening. While scrolling Pinterest I came across a quote that read:

"The moment you're about to give up is the moment right before the magic happens."

And I swear that was the penny-drop moment for me. With my background in copywriting and my experience in building two social media departments from the ground up, at two different companies, there was one thing I had seemed to have forgotten. I centred the social department's entire value proposition on **content strategy**. And at this company, *I* was the most qualified and experienced in content strategy. That's when I developed my next revenue-boosting idea for the business.

Breaking the glass ceiling

Content marketing means taking something a brand already has — like a website, brochure, press release, product demo, video, or even just an image — and reshaping it into useful content that speaks to different audiences. It's about repackaging one piece of source material into different forms of content, like a blog post, a social media post, an infographic, a how-to guide, etc. so that the brand shows up when people need it most.

In the age of social media, the one-size-fits-all approach does not work. The way people consume content on different digital platforms varies, and so the content that we serve people on all our brand touchpoints needs to be personalised to its audience. So instead of sharing a whitepaper, as it came, via different marketing channels like a website, blog and social media, think about repackaging the message of the whitepaper in different formats for different channels, depending on the audience viewing it. That is content marketing at its core. And if we go one step further, include data from Search to understand user behaviour, how they search for things, what they're searching for and when they are searching for it. This means we're able to create meaningful content that meet people where they are.

And because this strategy is based on data from search and social signals, the result is often highly targeted content that builds trust and inspires action.

Armed with only the notes I had scribbled in my notebook, I knocked on the glass door of our CEO's office.

"Do you have a minute?" I asked in my soft, apologetic tone that had not done me any favours throughout my career.

"Of course, Leilah. Come inside," He responded warmly.

And when we started talking about how things are, our weekend plans and how his dog, really our office dog, had left a surprise in one of the meeting rooms of our sister agencies, I was reminded of how fond I actually was of this man. I've always thought of him as the most approachable and genuine CEO and I felt a pang of disappointment for not making more of an effort recently to speak to him about what was really going on in the social department. I guess I was bitter because I thought everyone had just allowed my manager to treat me like a second-rate citizen, when in reality, no one probably knew.

And so I pitched him my spiel. My idea of this Content Marketing concept. The data bits, the marketing science bits, the content strategy bit. And of course, my vision for creating a Content Marketing department.

Now, back up a second. I didn't come up with this model all by myself. I had this notion of what Content Marketing should be, the idea of taking one piece of source content and tailoring it to different audiences who consume content in different ways on different platforms. I just wanted to create a department that planned content thoughtfully, that focused on surfacing the right content to people at the right time. I kept talking to everyone about my ideas and vision for this department. One person I discussed this with was my teammate, Mila, the head of Search. Over the years, SEO evolved into Search, which the industry felt was a more sophisticated term - the foundational concepts remained the same, more or less. Mila suggested we go one step further and include data from her team to understand user patterns, how they search for things and what they're searching for. It was her addition to my initial concept of Content Marketing that made my proposal robust and centred on performance. I was prepared to share the department with Mila, someone I trusted in the agency and highly respected. But she didn't want to be part of it, she was simply one of those sages who imparted wisdom and didn't necessarily need the credit for everything. She wanted me to pitch it, because when I got the go ahead, it meant that she would be relieved of the responsibility of sourcing content creators to support her team's Search strategy. It meant that we now had an in-house Content Marketing department who could do all that for her. It meant that she could finally focus solely on the Search strategy which is the part she loved. I was happy with that. Mila was happy with that. Win-win.

"It would be a new revenue stream for the business. And I could lead it." I chirped on to the CEO.

"Leilah this is fantastic. You've obviously put a lot of thought into this. And you know I love this, I don't always want to see a polished presentation on screen. This is great, Leilah."

There were many conversations after that, with many senior people. Logistics. Rate cards. Case studies. Pitch decks. Content Marketing was the new black, and all the account directors wanted in on it for their clients.

Of course I had an ulterior motive. I wanted out of the toxic manager situation, and this was my way out. I made a case for leading the department by myself, that I think it could scale, and that it shouldn't sit within the social department. In fact, I thought content marketing could fuel all departments where content was needed: social, search (organic and paid), media and web development. I'd start with the ongoing work I was already doing in social. I proposed to strip the social department down the middle and split out all the content strategy and content creation work, so that it now fell under the newly developed content marketing department where it belonged. Content marketing is the creative, the concept development, things I wanted to do when I wanted to make ads (social was still ads). Everything else, social channel strategy, the technical setup on social, community management, event coverage, measurement and reporting would stay within the social department. This seemed a logical and well thought-out plan, everyone agreed.

Meanwhile, the automobile brand spoiled us with great perks. As the sole content specialist working on the brand, I got first dibs when new vehicles launched in the country. The account director, client side, would set me up with keys to the launch model vehicle days before it hit showroom floors, asking me to drive it around Cape Town and make it Instagram famous. Back up... at the time, Instagram culture was big. I'm talking HUGE - [11]instawalks every weekend, a select few of Instagrammers running the scene, organising walks and creating campaigns for brands, and MJ and I were at the centre of it. This was outside of our day jobs. Instagram wasn't the polished influencer marketplace it would later become, but a playground for creatives, hobbyists, and urban explorers armed with nothing more than an iPhone and a love for light. Instagrammers - early adopters who lived and breathed the platform - weren't just posting pictures, we were building communities like IgersCapeTown, IgersJoburg, IgersDurban etc.

The feed was full of square crops, VSCO filters, and carefully composed shots of coffee cups, sneakers on patterned tiles, or sunlit city streets. Minimalism and symmetry reigned.

Instawalks captured the spirit of the time: groups of strangers meeting up in a city, walking with phones in hand, seeing the familiar through new eyes. These meetups were equal parts photography jam session and social bonding. People who had only known each other through usernames suddenly laughing together on rooftops, bridges, and alleyways.

---

[11] Photowalks, or social meet-ups, where a group of creatives come together to explore and capture parts of the city together, then share their images under a common hashtag on Instagram. In Cape Town, *instawalks* blended digital culture with local life — showcasing neighbourhoods, street art, and everyday beauty.

It was a moment when Instagram felt intimate yet expansive. Small enough that you could form real friendships through likes and comments, but big enough that a photo could ripple far beyond your circle. The culture was about curiosity, connection, and the joy of framing the world just so, not yet about followers as currency, but about being part of a shared visual conversation. I found a way to apply this to social creative for my clients, weaving in sponsored brand campaigns into this community. And that's why MJ and I got the keys to the latest sports cars almost every weekend. We returned the favour with beautifully composed shots of the gullwing doors glowing at sunsets on Chapman's Peak Drive - later shared by the global automobile brand.

In the end, I got the new title, head of content marketing, and the pay rise that came with it. The new title made me feel validated, and gave me a new sense of passion for work again. There was still that natural link between social and content but that didn't matter because I was no longer reporting into the same manager. The new social strategist, Camilla, my ex-manager's friend, who was supposed to come in and take all my clients from me, became one of my closest friends at the agency. She had this amazing sense of humour and would say things at the most stressful times that would crack me up. We both had the same passion for the brands we worked on, and for creative excellence. And without the baggage of my manager between us, everything felt a whole lot easier. We never spoke of my manager. I'm very sure her experience of being his direct report was very different to mine. And even if it wasn't, it was all part of the past now anyway. The glass ceiling was broken. For now.

Soaring, on a global scale

~ 2014 ~

The year before I moved to London. If I knew that 365 days later I would pack up my life in two suitcases and be living in another country, another continent, I would've chosen to work less and do more. Spend more time with my family, with my friends, with people I would probably not be able to see as often any more. But hindsight is 20/20.

Losing myself in work was just the distraction I needed to take my mind off of the grief that haunted me every day. My dad had his demons, but he was a good person. And towards the end of his life, he was really trying to be there for me. I felt a sense of guilt grieving him, because of other people's opinions of him, because of his relationship with my mum that wasn't perfect. I felt I needed permission to grieve, that I'd be letting my mum down if I felt any kind of sadness for him not being alive any more. But inside, it really hurt. So I shoved those feelings deep within me so it wouldn't touch the surface.

In a way, distracting myself from actually feeling anything was a way for me to get over the loss of my dad. Working all hours of the day, deciding to move to a different country; it was all one major distraction. I don't regret the decision, because it gave me the life we have now, which I would not trade for anything, but I do sometimes wish that I could do it over again, more thoughtfully, involve my family in the process, so that they had more time with me before we left.

With the new content marketing department, I was even busier at work than ever before. I created a new revenue stream for the business, and it came with all the accompanying financial admin as you'd imagine. Forecasting. Budgeting. Staffing. All the fun terms that didn't interest me at all. I wanted to focus on making great content, not running a small business. But it came with the territory.

When I formally started in my new role, it was all systems go. Nothing could stop me. I decided that I was quite good at finding the gaps in business and coming up with solutions for said gaps. Note to self, add that to my CV. The content marketing department focused on creative content development for social and digital channels. I worked closely with Camilla, who was now promoted to the head of social, creating integrated campaigns for social media.

My ex-manager moved on to the new business team. For what it's worth, I think he was a better fit for that team anyway; he was always really good at the pitch. When he left the department, Camilla thought that she had gotten the promotion by default, but I always believed that she earned it fair and square. She was an excellent strategist and an even better ally. She'd be the only person to call out a racist joke in a room where I'd just awkwardly laugh along. The more I got to know her, the more I admired her.

I thought back to all the times I closed myself up to her because of her association to my ex-manager and I regretted it deeply. She was nothing like him. We worked in unison. Together, we won so many client pitches for the agency. And prepping for a pitch with her felt less nerve-wracking. Her kind, welcoming personality brought a sense of camaraderie to the entire company. The culture had shifted, and Camilla was single-handedly responsible for that. I was still the only Coloured girl in the room when we pitched. But for a while, I felt like I belonged, like I was part of something. The dream team.

Pretty soon we had to hire more people because the work started flooding in and it was more work than the two of us could handle on our own. Camilla hired people. I hired people. My team of content creators were split across Cape Town and Johannesburg. It was a leadership decision. Most of our clients were in Johannesburg and having a content point of contact in Johannesburg was vital. Also, less money spent on flights. So now I was managing people remotely and it was a steep learning curve for me. I sometimes wondered if I were one of those garbage managers that I had at all the jobs before.

Recruiting and hiring was a new flex for me. I'd never done this before, but this agency trusted me to hire people and give them a permanent employment contract. Major. I googled interview questions to ask a content strategist, and found a surprisingly large number of resources. One common aspect of a copywriter or content strategist interview was to submit a copy test, to gauge the level of writing of each candidate. One candidate who applied for the job refused to do the copy test; instead they sent me a long, wordy email on all the reasons they thought that a copy test was beneath them, that they had years of experience and were overqualified for the job. I said okay, your call, you applied for the job. I read through dozens of beautiful copy test submissions from so many great candidates. I was inspired by their talent. One stood out for me. I knew from this candidate's copy test that they were the ideal person for the job. They had a way with words that I could only dream of. Their writing was enigmatic. I asked them to write about a new product launch, one piece of long form content and several post copy variations for social media. Alex submitted this and far beyond the task. And he became the first content strategist of the newly developed content marketing team. A star on the horizon.

The next person I needed to hire was meant to be based in Johannesburg. I couldn't be there in person, and at the time, I don't know why we never thought of using video conferencing calls. This was circa 2014, so Skype existed, right? Instead I was on the phone, interviewing someone blindly, while they sat in our Johannesburg office along with our chief commercial officer.

She interviewed well, and I loved all of her creative strategy answers. It also sounded like it came to her so effortlessly, unrehearsed. Our CCO agreed that she was the best candidate. But he also told me to think deeply about who I hire in this position. Though she interviewed well, she seemed ambitious, like she wouldn't want to stay in this role for long, and that might mean that she would come after my job. Those types of things happened in the industry in South Africa; I've heard too many stories, our CCO was right. But also, I wanted to be around people who were better than me, people who I could learn from and take inspiration from. I wanted to create a team that exuded creative excellence. And I couldn't do that if I said no to hiring brilliant people. I knew in my gut that she was the right person. So Aimee became the second content strategist of the content marketing team and the first Johannesburg-based creative. I didn't care if she maybe one day would come for my job; I wanted to work with people who were exceptional and hungry and curious, and Aimee was all of that and more.

Towards the end of that quarter, I won an award for my individual contribution to the company. The award celebrated people who *do the extraordinary, ask more of themselves than others do, who believe excellence is an attitude and who want the hallmark of excellence.* There were 400+ people at the agency, and they gave the award to me. It was easy for me to believe that I didn't deserve the award, that other people were more worthy of winning than I was. But then I thought about everything I achieved in that year; founding a new department, designing a brand new product offering, hiring a team of specialists, becoming a people manager, building ongoing-revenue for the business. It sure deserved something. Coloured girl moving up in the world, I thought.

My mum was proud. The award came with a life-sized cheque of R20 000 that my mum still keeps stashed behind the living room sofa. I used the actual money to book a trip to Vietnam for MJ and I, and it was on this trip where I met the person whose flat I stayed at when I was almost homeless in London.

Shortly after the award, I was elected to be part of the global steering board for the agency. Iridium was part of a global network of agencies with offices all around the globe, including London. Word had gotten out around the network about the work we were doing in Cape Town with content marketing, and the product specialists across the globe wanted to scale this product. They wanted to use my content marketing blueprint and take it global. Yeah baby.

The exact quote on my invitation letter read:

```
"We based the leadership group on executive
interviews, vendor recommendations, and peer
reviews. You were one of the few that have been hand
selected to drive innovation globally for our
agency."
```

Gratitude was never too far from my daily thoughts. Enjoy the highs, I kept saying to myself. Because they don't last forever. Life comes in seasons, and we should appreciate the highs and lows equally. But equally, every time something good happened to me, I asked myself, was this a replacement blessing because the loss of my dad was so big?

Imposter syndrome enters the chat

As a global steering board appointee, my role at Iridium stretched in every direction I could imagine. On top of my daily duties as head of content marketing, I was also responsible for service definitions, defining what our product offering looked like in every market, identifying global vendors that we'd establish partnerships with, taking ownership and driving the agency's official point of view on industry changes and news, creating and running webinars, global testing and planning among other things. It was intense. It also meant a substantial amount of late nights. We spent hours streamlining the content marketing product, ensuring that the service we offer in any of our other markets is consistent with what we offered in South Africa. And one of the offices I got to collaborate with in the steering group, was Iridium London, UK.

I was the head of content marketing at this agency with a global footprint. I was influencing what content marketing as a service looked like for all our agencies, globally. And I was winning awards for creative excellence while doing it. On paper I was excelling in my career, so why was I still so depressed inside? The job, even though fulfilling, was stressing me out for sure. I was spending way too much time working. All the late nights at the office, followed by long nights and weekends where I continued to work at home. The job required it. I had no time to switch off. Signs of burnout were creeping in. And even though I was producing the best work I've ever done, I still worried about losing my job every single day. Imposter syndrome, I've been told, is when an individual doubts their skills, expertise and achievements and has an internalised fear of being exposed as a fraud. Despite real evidence of competence, people with imposter syndrome don't believe that their success is warranted. As people of colour, imposter syndrome hits a little harder. And as a woman of colour in a predominantly White industry, imposter syndrome hit even harder. I always felt that I wasn't good enough for the advertising and marketing world. I didn't go to a pedigree Ad School; I didn't have any ad agency or creative agency background. I was just a hard-working Coloured girl. I didn't feel acknowledged. I didn't feel like I could speak up in a brainstorm or in meetings. I never wanted to present my own ideas. Even though I was capable and talented, I didn't believe in myself. The lack of representation of people of colour in the industry amplifies these types of feelings. As psychologist Emily Hu once said, *"We're more likely to experience imposter syndrome if we don't see many examples of people who look like us or share our background who are clearly succeeding in our field."*

Born in a system that oppressed people of colour, I was led to believe that I'm not worthy of the same opportunities that my White peers had access to. I believed that I wasn't deserving of the success that came as a result of access to those opportunities. So when success happened for me, and when success happens for us, despite our circumstances and because of the narrative drilled into our heads by an apartheid government, we start to feel like an imposter. Imposter syndrome enters the chat. Though there has been significant progress in the industry when it comes to diversity and inclusion, people of colour are still under-represented in leadership positions, and also in the makeup of creative teams. There are even fewer women of colour taking up space in the creative, media and tech industries. The lack of role models in these industries, for women of colour, are few and far between and this contributes to us feeling like we don't belong.

And then there's the flip side, feeling imposter syndrome as a result of a company's diversity, equity and inclusion efforts. I don't know how many times it crossed my mind if I was the diversity hire. If maybe I was only hired for the colour of my skin, my ethnicity or my gender and not for my ability to do the job.

When you're dealing with all of this emotional baggage, you end up with the need to constantly prove yourself, which is what I experienced. I pushed myself harder and harder and eventually set a benchmark for what my manager and peers can expect from me. If I delivered under this benchmark, it would look like I was underperforming. And if I continued to perform at or above the benchmark, I was at risk of burning out and fast. I felt like I was burning out at Iridium. I was also still trying to live with the grief of losing my dad, and making peace with the relationship we never had. It left me in an uncomfortable space, where on paper everything looked on track but internally there was a misalignment. I knew something had to change to get me out of this rut, but I wasn't yet sure how.

You don't get what you don't ask for

"What's up, Nate, how's it going?" I casually asked into the conference phone in the meeting room. Sirens blared in the background on the other side of the call. "Is everything alright?"

"Haha, yeah, that's standard in London. Sirens every five minutes if you're near the city." Nate responded. "But actually, yeah this week's been pretty good. We've made huge progress with all the stuff you sent over, so thank you massively for that."

"Ah cool, I'm glad it helped."

"Massively," he insisted.

We continued talking about the rest of the plans for the content marketing product and decided that I'd present some of our case studies at the next global steering group all-hands meeting.

"The work you're doing sounds really cool," I said as we reached the end of the meeting agenda, "I wish *we* got client briefs like that."

"Well," Nate said, "If you were in London, you'd get to work on all these client briefs."

"Haha, really?"

"Yeah, really. We'd love to have someone like you on the team."

"And you'd hire someone from South Africa, to come over there? Don't you have loads of content people in London?" I mused.

"Yes, we have a big content team. We're starting to build it out a bit more, hiring more creative specialists, people like you. You'd be a good fit here."

That evening I drove home with many questions on my mind. I passed through Woodstock Main Road, onto Settler's Way and cut onto the M3 highway. Blink182's *Neighbourhoods* blasting through my Clio's music player. At 8:05pm the peak hour traffic had thinned out. I was cruising, pretending I was drifting in that black Mercedes-Benz SLS with gullwing doors; the one I got to drive at our team building event earlier that month at the Kyalami race track.

Was Nate serious? Could I really entertain the idea of moving to London, the creative hub of the world? Hmm, maybe, I thought excitedly. London, what an interesting idea. Could I really make it there? Would MJ want to move there? And what would our families think? At dinner that night I told MJ and my mum about the call.

"But what about Sutro?" MJ asks.

Through all the excitement and hullabaloo, it completely slipped my mind that two months earlier, MJ and I had adopted a baby Chow Chow, Sutro. She was a 3-month-old, red Chow Chow puppy. A double-coated teddy bear with a purple tongue. We adopted her from a family in Athlone where they called her Fergie. She was the runt of the litter, the smallest baby, all her brothers and sisters were already on their way to their furever homes. No one wanted Fergie. She was smaller than her brothers and sisters and didn't have your typical Chow Chow flat face. We fell in love with her instantly, and we couldn't leave without her. So we brought her home and named her Sutro, after the Instagram filter. It suited her more.

Of course, we couldn't go to London. Of course I couldn't entertain this crazy idea any more. Our lives were here in Cape Town, with Sutro. There was no way we would leave the country without her. That was final.

"Oh my God, no! I forgot about Sutro for a minute. No, we won't go. Simple as that." I said.

"Yeah, we can't leave her," MJ agreed.

"You know, lots of people emigrate and take their pets with them." My mum piped up.

"Hmm." MJ and I responded at the same time, as we digested

this new information.

When people plan to move away from their home country, months and months of planning goes into it. Years even. MJ and I had barely even mentioned the idea of emigrating to each other, let alone anyone else. It sure as hell had never even crossed my mind before this phone call with Nate. Leaving Cape Town for pastures new was something other people did. With our blue flag beaches, the majestic Table Mountain and all that natural beauty; I was living in the best city in the world.

But it was an idea. A suggestion from Nate. And I wasn't opposed to the idea. Maybe it was something I could want? I don't know. Everything was very conceptual and uncertain. There were too many unanswered questions and details that we needed to discuss. Neither of us had even been to London on a holiday. We knew nothing about the city, except from what we saw on TV. We ended the evening conversations saying that the idea was not completely off the table. And if it came down to Sutro or London, we would choose Sutro, obviously. I decided to do some research about moving abroad with a dog. I also decided to email Nate, probing more into what he said about me being in the London office. What would it look like? How would it work? He replied almost instantly:

```
Speak to these people. Tell them you're interested.
I'll introduce you.

N.
```

The interview

It was a Thursday afternoon. I had a phone interview scheduled for 3p.m Greenwich Mean Time, which meant an hour later in Cape Town, with the head of media at Iridium London. I took the day off, I prepped all week, I made sure my phone was charged and I waited for the call. 3p.m came, no call. 3:15 rolled on, still no call. 3:25 came and I decided to call them - no answer. Maybe this was just too good to be true, I thought.

Before giving up on the prospect of it all, I wrote an email to the head of media, asking if I'd gotten the time mixed up because of the time zone difference. I knew I hadn't, but it was easier to play it this way instead of asking him straight out why he stood me up. I apologised and asked if it were at all possible to reschedule. He responded, apologising profusely. He had a meeting that had run over and lost track of time. We rescheduled. Yes! We rescheduled! It was still on.

When I eventually had the call, I thought I blew it. I didn't have answers for any of the questions he asked me, and he didn't ask me any of the questions that I had prepared answers for. It was a colossal mess. Maybe this is what a London interview is like? Maybe I got the prep work all wrong? I knew nothing would come of this. I wanted the call to end, to put myself out of this misery of awkwardness.

"Alright, great. Well, I think you should speak to our head of research and development as well. He's building out a creative team at the minute and he'd be a good person to speak to." The head of media said.

"Ah thank you," I responded in a higher-pitched voice than usual.

"Yes, his name is AW and I'll put you in touch via email. Alright, good to speak. Cheers, bye."

I left the call feeling very confused. I absolutely thought that I blew it. But this guy wanted me to meet someone else too? A follow-up interview? Did I make it to the second stage? Did I pass the screening?

The period after that was equally confusing. Weeks and weeks went by after that call and nothing happened. I didn't want to seem too desperate, or just desperate at all, so I didn't follow up. I left it alone while I compulsively checked my email every 10 minutes for an update. A ping. A red dot above my mail app icon. Anything to see the glorious sight of a new email appearing in my inbox, subject line in bold: London opportunity.

Meanwhile, I had forgotten that our account director had submitted a bunch of our summer content campaigns for several national and international awards. I'd written the summaries for the campaigns, but didn't expect to win anything. The awards scene was cut-throat. We usually competed with pure, traditional creative agencies and as a digital performance agency, our briefs didn't really align with many of the categories that awards organisations were looking for. I got an email. Not the email I was waiting for, but an equally good email. We won an award for the automobile brand; best in class for digital marketing. A performance marketing campaign? Won a creative excellence award? I could not fathom it. Then, a few seconds later, another email. Another award. Wow, this was great. Two awards, I was beyond happy with that. Then another. And another. The alerts kept coming in for all the awards we'd won. Silver, gold, bronze, we won them all. 23 Awards in total. In that blast of various email alerts, one of them stood out. Gold for Best Use of Content. Best Use of Content in a Social Campaign. I'm sorry, what? Though I knew my work was somewhat related to the list of 23 awards that had just come in, this one was different. This one was validation. This one was *Best Use of Content*. This was my vision for content marketing coming true, and it meant everything to me.

The judges thought it was:

```
"A brilliant example of a well-thought through
content campaign, based on smart insights and
leveraging the entire bought, owned and earned media
ecosystem. Very effective for the client and one to
be shared around the network."
```

Everyone in the Iridium network, including the London office, saw it. It was the first Gold of the evening, and the first Gold for South Africa. Then two weeks after the awards announcement, I got the call I was waiting for.

AW, the head of research and development, was a lovely man. We spoke for an hour about all the work I'd done, and why I chose this industry. He told me his reasons too. It felt like having a conversation with an old friend.

"So, tell me, is it at all possible that you guys would even think about hiring someone from South Africa for your creative team?" I felt comfortable enough to ask.

"Oh, yes of course! Forgive me, I thought that had been covered already. I didn't realise it was so unclear. Yes, we want you to come to London to join the team," AW spoke the words that gave me the reassurance I needed to start making solid plans.

There was no role available per se. But they were going to create a role for me, because they wanted me on their team, and they would also help with my and MJ's visa. By then, MJ and I had made the decision that if London called, we'd answer. And Sutro was coming with us, thanks to Animal Travel Services who specialised in transporting pets across countries safely and ethically. If Sutro couldn't receive first-class treatment in a 13 hour flight from Cape Town to London, we would forgo the whole damn idea. And that was our deal-breaker. We wouldn't have it any other way.

Circus Charlie and visa applications

For most South Africans, when you get that confirmation of an international company offering you a job, the rest is pretty simple. I have a couple of friends who moved over on ancestral visas; they had family ties in Britain and could therefore obtain a visa by right of ancestry. But for those of us without ancestry in the United Kingdom - the brown ones, as it were - the road ahead was much harder. For this reason, the job offer was made conditional: if I were not granted a visa, the offer would be withdrawn. For us, to get a visa which allowed us to live and work in the United Kingdom, there was only one truly feasible route, the skilled worker visa. And even this route was not guaranteed to be successful.

The most common UK visas (very loosely explained) are:

- **Spousal visa**: If your partner is of British descent, you as a South African can apply for a spousal visa by way of marriage and you get to live and work in the United Kingdom without any restrictions. You can also get a Spousal visa if your partner has any legitimate visa to live and work in the UK.
- **Ancestral visa:** If you can prove that one of your grandpar-

ents was born in the United Kingdom, the Channel Islands or the Isle of Man, you can apply for an ancestral visa.
- **Skilled worker visa (previously known as a Tier 2 visa):** If you've received a job offer from an employer with an office in the United Kingdom, and the employer has been approved by the Home Office. The Home Office is also known as Home Affairs and oversees all immigration business.

There are several other types of visas that you can obtain to gain clearance to enter the UK, for example specialist job visas like the Health and Care Worker visa, Minister of Religion visa, but naturally, as a copywriter, I couldn't apply for any of those visas. My job was a different specialism. The skilled worker visa requires one to jump through hoops of fire like you're on level 5 of Circus Charlie. And once you've completed the level, the final decision still sits with the Home Office. It could go either way for you.

A skilled worker visa is a sponsorship from a company who wants to hire you. The sponsorship is not monetary, though there are hefty fees involved for the sponsor, the sponsorship is a declaration to the Home Office that the company has done due diligence and supports your application to enter the country. Not all companies are able to sponsor foreign workers. Companies need to apply for a sponsor licence, in order to get permission to employ foreign workers. To get a sponsor licence, there are several admin things companies need to do to prove that they are able to employ foreign workers.

Iridium had offices across the globe, which meant they were

already employing a diverse range of expats in all of their offices. They didn't need to apply for a sponsor licence, as they already had one. But they did need to advertise the job - my job - publicly for a couple of weeks before they could offer it to me, officially. And while the job was posted publicly, anyone could apply for the job, my job, and would be granted a fair chance to interview. As part of the process, Iridium needed to interview all applicants who applied for my job, and were required to make notes that would be submitted to the Home Office on each applicant's interview. They needed to prove to the Home Office why, after interviewing several candidates, they still felt that I was a better fit for the role. They needed to prove that I was an exceptional candidate and they couldn't find anyone else, who perhaps didn't need a visa, to fill the role. They needed to prove that I was more qualified and experienced that anyone from within the local talent pool in the United Kingdom and Europe. Only if the Home Office deemed the evidence and case acceptable, would they grant a certificate of sponsorship (CoS). A magic series of numbers that would change the course of my career and life.

During the external interview process, there were numerous times when I thought that Iridium would find someone else who would be a better fit for the role. I spent several weeks in limbo, waiting to hear back.

After Iridium's immigration lawyers explained the process to me, I didn't have much confidence that everything would work out and we would be able to go to London after all. I mean surely they'd find someone that was already in London that could do my job. How would they prove that I was exceptional? I was just a Coloured girl from Wynberg, with no university degree. AW told me that the job was mine, but it was all still dependent on the visa. And so I didn't tell my family that we were moving to London because the chance of the move materialising was slim. The only person who knew was my mum.

MJ, my mum and I spent a great many weeks playing the *what would we do if we moved to London?* game. We'd explore neighbourhoods on Google maps, deciding where we'd want to live, where we'd want to eat, where we'd walk Sutro and what we'd do on the weekends. Our game felt like nothing more but a game, a dream that wouldn't materialise.

"Don't you think you should tell your aunties?" My mum asked me one day, as we strolled through the Cape Town night market that opened for the festive season.

"But what if I jinx it by talking about it?" I asked.

In December 2014, the Certificate of Sponsorship was granted. This meant I could finally apply for my visa as well as MJ's visa, as an extension of mine. I exhausted all of my savings to pay for our visa applications, somewhere upwards of £2,500 per person, because we used the priority service. The standard service was a bit more affordable, but we weren't prepared to wait six months for a decision to be made. Iridium wanted me to start as soon as possible, so we decided to use the priority service. I also had an irrational fear that if I waited too long, I'd lose the visa and the sponsorship completely. The previous weeks spent in limbo were more than both of us could handle.

Then the never-ending expenses started that came with a big move like this one. We needed a chest x-ray for the Tuberculosis test; we couldn't enter the UK without one, because we were from Africa where apparently TB was rife? I had no idea. We also needed to pass a Grade 2-level English exam to demonstrate our understanding of the English language. Our final application pack was larger than any thesis ever written, and our entire future hinged on it.

* * *

The familiar sights of Lanseria airport at sunrise settled my somewhat anxious brain as I walked through arrivals towards the car hire bays. Flying to and from our Johannesburg office every second week had become the norm for me since I created my new role as head of content marketing. I now had a team and clients in two cities, and that required me to be there physically to some degree. The routine was predictable, the early morning flights, the takeaway blueberry muffin and latte that I called breakfast, rushing to the departure gate because I was always late. Then the interrupted sleep I'd try to fit in on the plane to make up for waking up at 3am for the airport. But no one gets any sleep in economy class.

That day would ultimately be the last time I visited the Joburg office. With the visa application underway, and my move being more or less confirmed, I was planning to share the official news with the team that day. I had a meeting scheduled with our chief commercial officer (CCO) first, and then I'd informally and confidentially share with my immediate team. My manager was already in the loop as AW wanted to speak to him as part of the interview process. Even though Iridium was an agency with offices around the globe, the South African offices still felt small and like a family. I was fond of our CCO and CEO - the duo who started the South African business all those years ago. I felt a little nervous breaking the news to them. How would they react? I wondered.

The morning before the meeting with the CCO, I didn't get any work done; aimlessly switching between tabs on my browser, wanting the clock to count down.

"Howzit?" The CCO said in his warm, welcoming way.

"I'm alright. How're you?" I replied as I sat across the desk in his office.

"Hmf. Always busy," he laughed.

"I appreciate you making the time. So I'll get straight into it."

"Please,"

"This is really hard for me to say, and it might not be definite yet, but I have to let you know.. I'm pursuing a position in our London office," I said, gingerly.

"When you say you're pursuing, do you mean you've applied and are waiting to hear back?" He asked.

"It's not that formal. I just reached out to the team in the UK and asked if it even was a possibility. And the conversations from there seem positive." I said. "They said they'd be open to creating a role for me."

"Wow, Leilah, that's a great testament to the work that you've been doing here. How far along is the process? How did this happen?" He asked.

I filled him in on all the details that led up to me being able to say that I was considering accepting a job in London. The nerves immediately turned to excitement as I got the initial news out of the way. I tried to play it down, to make it seem like it was nothing. Like nothing was confirmed yet. That I was still waiting for my visa. The last part was true.

He listened as I apologised for finding a better opportunity. He listened as I said I didn't want to abandon them, but an opportunity like this wouldn't fall into my lap twice. He listened as I spoke about how passionate I was about the little department I was building and how I was influencing the content marketing industry in South Africa. He also gave me advice on how to handle the next few months at the agency, how to plan my transition. And as we sat and spoke about all the possibilities that would come from a move like this, I still didn't believe it myself that this would actually happen for me.

This is a Piccadilly line service to...Cockfosters

~2015~

In January 2015 I got the official job offer, content director at Iridium London, though all the paperwork proves that it came through weeks before then. Excellent. It was actually happening. We were going to London. The visas were just a page in our green passports, and I wondered what all the fuss and money was about. I guess I expected something more glorious than a piece of paper.

MJ and I immediately launched into the large volume of planning and preparation needed in order for the three of us to emigrate. Even after all the immigration madness that we managed to get through, if there was still no safe and ethical way for Sutro to join us in London, we just wouldn't go. We would give up our visas, it was that simple. But MJ found a company called Animal Travel Services and they met all our requirements, so we trusted them with Sutro. Time was moving fast and we needed to sort our flights, accommodation and try to save some money for food during our first month in London. Everyone always talks about London being the place where you can be anyone, anything you want. That was the promise we were holding on to. It was what I was holding on to. I wanted to be someone else, in a new city, and forget all about the broken person I was in the place where I grew up.

The timing for MJ was not ideal. He'd just started a new job in the tech team at one of South Africa's major retailers and his career was on the up. He was exactly where he wanted to be, and here I was asking him to come to London with me. I felt guilty asking him to give up everything. For me it was a simple decision, I wanted to get away. But for him, I guess he had a lot more to give up. I was yearning for a fresh start away from everything that was causing me pain. But for him, he was taking a chance on the unknown. For me I was running away, for him, he was running towards. I hope London will be kind to us, I thought.

The remainder of that quarter I pushed myself even harder at work. I built the content marketing department from the ground up. I wanted to leave it in good shape so that it could continue even after I left. My handover was long and tedious. I made notes of everything I'd done since the inception of content marketing at Iridium, from designing the value proposition, defining our SLAs, all the pitch collateral, the processes, the templates, ideas that I saved in the idea bank. I was determined to not let content marketing at the agency disappear. And so those last few months from when I told them about London, my entire focus was my handover, and training my team to take on some of my leadership and strategic responsibilities. My manager decided that the business would not replace me as head of content marketing. I honestly didn't know if I should feel offended or elated about that. Offended that they thought that I wasn't worth replacing, that my work could be absorbed by the rest of the team and didn't need a whole person. And elated because I didn't need to spend my last few weeks at the agency onboarding someone completely new.

I mapped out my transition plan and sent it to my manager. I figured as a manager, he'd find it helpful. But instead he found it an opportunity to tell me that I couldn't leave the company when I planned to.

```
Hi Leilah
That does not work. According to our employment
contracts, we are all bound by a two month notice.
So legally, you would have to resign first and then
work in your two months notice. This would give us
enough time to plan for your replacement.
```

I stared at the email in disbelief. Was this man just consciously disregarding all our communication in the last six months? We'd openly and exhaustively discussed the fact that because it is an inter-company transfer, I wouldn't be resigning. I'd just plan a handover to my team. He also announced it in our team meeting that they wouldn't hire anyone to replace me. I found that last line in his email preposterous. I was livid.

Throughout my time working under my manager's leadership, I felt undervalued. I felt more valued by other leaders outside of my immediate team. Other business unit leaders recognised my value, but not my own manager. I never once complained about this, because it wasn't important to me. I enjoyed the autonomy and the validation from the rest of the business. That gave me a signal that I was doing work that influenced the success of the business. The response to my transition plan from my manager felt like the last straw.

I vented about this newfound information to my close friends at the agency; mostly I asked for advice. It was then when I discovered that during staff pay rise discussions, my manager actively blocked a pay rise for me. The CFO had budgeted an amount for everyone's standard salary increases, and my manager insisted that I didn't need that much of an increase, that I could go with less. Allegedly, of course. This is all hearsay, but I trusted the source, they had no reason to make it up. The information was also useless to me at the time, as I was exiting the company. But it did tell me a whole lot about the type of person my manager really was. And another reason confirming why moving was the right decision for me.

In his defence, I remember once jokingly telling my manager that I wasn't in it for the money, that I just wanted to do great work and the money was a bonus that I get to do what I love. In retrospect, I should never have said that to my manager. As a Coloured girl in a predominantly White industry in South Africa, I should not have said that to anyone. I should have advocated for myself. For my worth. For the value I was bringing to the business. Because clearly, no one else was advocating for me, not even the one person I expected to have my back in the workplace.

But brown culture trains us to be grateful for everything. Don't ask for anything more because you might ruin what you already have. Just be grateful. Keep your head down, and you'll get what you want. The opposite is true for my White colleagues: they learned that asking for what they wanted often got them exactly that. Standing up for yourself, making sure people know your worth by vocalising it is what gets you noticed. What doesn't get you noticed is keeping your head down and being grateful for everything. In my late 20s, I was only starting to learn this lesson now. And what a valuable lesson it was.

* * *

In April 2015, a day before my wedding anniversary, I said goodbye to MJ, Sutro and my family at the Cape Town International airport. The plan was for me to leave for London first, get our accommodation sorted and MJ would fly over a few weeks later with Sutro. Dogs weren't allowed to travel without a companion and since I needed to start work immediately, we decided that Sutro's travel companion would be MJ. To say it was stressful is putting it mildly. It took every fibre of my being to remain calm and not overthink about all the ways it could go wrong on that 13-hour flight for my fur child. I prayed and prayed and prayed for MJ and Sutro's safe travel across the border. I knew MJ would be fine. It was gentle little soft-hearted Sutro that I was worried about. I wished I could be there to explain to her what was happening when they asked her to get into a crate. I tried to get my hands on everything about animals migrating with their owners to feed my reassurance. I chose to have faith and believe that it would all be okay. Because it was the only way I could continue this mad adventure.

I wrapped my arms around my aunts, my cousins, my friends, and finally my mum — all of them gathered at the airport to say goodbye. Their faces carried a heavy sadness, and I felt it too, like a weight pressing down on my chest. But beneath that sorrow was something else - a flicker of relief. Relief at finally being able to pack this part of my life into a box, to step away from the version of me that had carried so much baggage, too heavy, too painful to keep dragging forward.

Out of the corner of my eye, I saw my dad in the background, or rather the ghost of him standing there as he always had, distanced, distracted, never quite present. In my mind he gives me a nod as I head toward security. And I can't help but wonder: what would he have thought of my plan to start over in a new city? Would this moment even exist if he were still alive? Probably not. If he were still alive, I might not have felt the urge to escape, to tear myself away. But he wasn't. And because he wasn't, I did.

* * *

Thirteen hours later, I was heading out of the back of the plane at Heathrow International airport. The plane was stuffy. I had sleep in my eyes and my mouth was dry. I was sitting at a window seat, which meant that I would be one of the last people to leave the plane. Still, I attempted to get up, hovered above my seat, indicating to the people next to me to move ahead so I too could stand in the aisle and wait to be let out of this gigantic metal tube. I turned on my phone, knowing that I wouldn't have signal as my network died when we crossed the African border. Just like that I was in another time zone. Here. On London soil. I had this picture in my head of how I thought it would be; I'd stand in the arrivals hall of the airport, the swing doors would open and I'd see a glimpse of the outside and think to myself, *this is home*. But the picture in your head of how something is supposed to be is never quite how it actually is.

When I reached the end of the movable stairway, a uniformed man held up a sign with my name on it. But I didn't order a taxi? Maybe the agency sent someone to collect me?

"Hi, that's me," I said as I approached the man in uniform.

"Ma'am, you need to come with me. Your luggage has been lost in flight and you need to fill out a form with my colleague at the desk."

He spoke so fast, I almost didn't hear everything he said.

Did he just say that my luggage was lost? My first day in a new city, a new country, and I wouldn't have a toothbrush. This is off to a great start, I thought. I followed the uniformed man to a makeshift desk in the middle of baggage claim. I filled out some forms at the desk, remembering to give my work address as I wasn't sure where I'd be staying yet. I had the AirBnB for the next three days but I was hoping to find a more permanent rental to move to after that. When I completed the paperwork, I exited the baggage claim hall and entered the roped aisles for border control. A woman behind a desk examined my passport and while flipping through the pages, she asked if I was a visitor or a resident.

"I don't know," I responded. "It's my first day in the UK, and I start a new job tomorrow."

She paged through my passport, looking for a very specific page, my visa.

"Okay, you're on a Tier 2 visa, so you're a resident. Do you have any family here? Or friends?" She smiled, looking up at me.

"No."

"Well you'll make friends in no time, don't worry." She stamped my passport and handed it back to me.

Heathrow airport was busy. I tried to find my way through the crowd, looking for the London Underground. I already mapped my route from the airport to the AirBnB in Hammersmith. Trying to navigate my way through an unknown airport without any luggage felt easier than I thought. I immediately remember to thank God for small glories. I spotted the entrance to the Underground. I could see the platform from where I was standing in the hallway, the metal turnstiles acting as the only barrier to entry. I located the ticket counter and asked the woman at the counter if this was where I could load money on my Oyster card, gifted to me by Katy from media planning.

"How much?" She asked.

"Um, I don't know. I need to get to Hammersmith."

"I'll put £5," She said while typing something on her computer.

I paid for my travel fare and asked, "How do I get to the other side?"

"What?" She yelled from behind the glass of the ticket counter.

"It's my first day here. How do I get to the train?" I asked self-consciously.

"It's just there! Just tap your card on the yellow reader and go through!" She yelled and pointed ahead.

"Thank you."

It worked just like she said. I tapped my Oyster card on the yellow reader at the turnstile and the metal gates swung open for a brief moment, leaving just enough time for me to pass through. The platform was empty. There was an electronic board displaying words, but I wasn't sure what it meant. Names of places maybe? The edge of the platform was lined with a thick, bright yellow line with the words MIND THE GAP painted just in front of it. I've heard this iconic line over and over before; seeing it in person was a surreal moment for me. Somewhere on the platform a loudspeaker went off and someone announced, "The next train to Cockfosters will arrive in two minutes. Please mind the gap between the train and the platform." *Ah, so that's what it meant*, I thought.

A girl appeared on the platform next to me. She was dressed in jeans and a leather jacket, her dark hair hanging loosely in her face. She looked like someone you'd meet in Cape Town — approachable. So I went over and asked,

"Hey, have you done this before?"

She looked at me without smiling, urging me to elaborate on my question.

"Can you help me? I need to get to Hammersmith." I eventually asked.

"Um, yeah just get on any tube, they're all going that way." She said, again without smiling back.

"Oh, any one?" I asked.

The girl nodded without looking up from her phone.

Okay then. My first few encounters with people from London were also not what I expected. It was cold and unfriendly, apart from the lovely officer at border control. I suddenly realised how alone I was in this big city, and I worried if I'd be able to make it on my own while MJ was still in Cape Town. A red, blue and white train pulled up at the platform at bullet speed interrupting my thoughts. A rush of air blew my hair in all directions and suddenly the platform turned to chaos. The train doors automatically slid open and people were getting off the train. The woman on the speaker announced again, "This is a Piccadilly Line Service to Cockfosters, the next station is Heathrow Terminal 2 and 3. Please keep all your personal belongings with you at all times."

I stepped inside the train and took a seat at the far end. I logged this in my mental notebook as my very first experience of the tube in London. Everything about it overwhelmed me. The tube map, the names on the digital boards, the announcements; it was all confusing. And why was everything so fast-paced? It seemed like there was no time to stop to take a breath. I tried to gather my thoughts and calm myself as I studied the tube map I had folded in my pocket. The Piccadilly line went directly to Hammersmith, where my AirBnB was, so I just needed to pay close attention to the boards on the platforms every time the tube stopped. *If* I was even on the Piccadilly line right now. Only time would tell. There were many stations before Hammersmith: Hatton Cross, Hounslow West, Hounslow Central, Hounslow East and so forth. I listened to the voice on the announcements at every station as we passed it. "The next station is Hatton Cross." Phew. I was on the right train at least.

The tube went underground for long periods of time and all I could see were flashes of blackness through the windows. When it emerged back overground I could make out a few brown brick buildings in what looked like a residential area. It looked extremely unremarkable. Not the London I saw on TV. No red telephone booths, no bright city lights, no hustle and bustle. Where the hell was I?

I traced my finger on the navy blue line from Heathrow to Hammersmith on the paper tube map I grabbed from the kiosks at Heathrow airport. *Not far to go now*, I thought. Throughout the journey I noticed that the doors only opened for a brief minute before shutting again and that made me a little anxious. Would I make it out on time? And if I don't, would I be able to get back to Hammersmith if I missed the stop?

When the tube eventually reached Hammersmith, I grabbed my handbag and tried to make it out the doors as quickly as it opened. I didn't know exactly where to go, so on a whim I decided to follow the people who left the train with me. I felt compelled to pick up my pace and walk as fast as everyone else, but soon found myself out of breath. As I exited the turnstiles, using the same Oyster tap method as I'd done when I entered, I noticed a cellphone shop with blue branding. I walked towards it and the first item I bought on UK soil was a UK-network SIM card. Hello Lebara.

A matchbox in Notting Hill

Hammersmith is a lovely neighbourhood. I found the AirBnB just above the Distillery pub. I went inside to check in and check out the space. All I wanted to do was take a long nap on the comfy sofa in the open-plan living room, but I forced myself to stay awake because there were a gazillion things I needed to do before MJ and Sutro arrived. I tried to orientate myself. *Food first*, I thought. I went downstairs and took a walk down the street to a mini mart I noticed on my way to the AirBnB earlier. Londis. I scanned the prices of everything as I slowly made my way down each aisle. I decided to buy just the bare essentials: white bread, American cheese slices, an avocado, orange juice. Back at the AirBnB I inserted the new SIM card to my phone and connected to the apartment WiFi to catch up on messages.

With my entire luggage missing, I had no clothes for work. I remembered that while chatting to my cousin in the United Arab Emirates - where she teaches English - she mentioned that I could pick up some affordable clothes at Primark stores in London. So I went online to search for the nearest Primark. Luckily, there was one right on King's Road, a few blocks from the AirBnB, and I managed to find a pair of jeans for £4. *This will have to do for now,* I thought. It was all the money I could afford to spend. I made another mental note of the store name as a place I'd like to come back to when I do eventually make more money.

Alone and confused and back in the comforts of the AirBnB, I tried to make some headway with finding a rental. First I called the specialist letting agency who focused on finding rentals for tenants with pets. They promised a full day of viewings and at the end of the day I'd find permanent accommodation. With no time to waste, I figured this was my best option.

"Great, so we'll just need you to deposit the £3500 and then we can start our search for you." The woman's voice was crisp over the line.

There was a long pause.

"I'm sorry?" I asked, half-wondering if I'd misheard her.

"Just the deposit of £3,500, for now."

"Oh. Um.. I can't. Um, I'm sorry, the deposit?"

"Yes, and then upon confirmation of your lease, you can pay the remaining £5000,"

The numbers landed like stones in my chest. "Oh. I'm sorry. I don't have that much," I admitted, my voice shrinking.

"How much do you have, and we can work around that," Her tone softened, almost coaxing.

I stared down at my notebook where I'd scrawled "flat hunting" in hopeful, looping letters "I...I only have the first month's rent I think, £1000?"

"Honey, that's not enough for a two-bed garden flat."

The words knocked the air out of me. "Oh…" The word caught in my throat. Tears pressed at the back of my eyes. "I'm so sorry I wasted your time."

"Don't be silly. Don't worry about that. Listen, is it your first time in London?" she asked.

"It's my first day,"

"Okay, listen. I'm going to transfer back your registration fee, so you have some more to play with while you figure things out, okay?" she said, "And don't worry, you'll figure it out."

I pressed the phone harder to my ear, as if that might hold me together. "Okay. Thank you."

I was starting to realise that I didn't do enough planning before arriving in the big city. I clearly didn't have enough money to get us settled. I needed to be smart and thrifty. I was relying on this specialist agency to find us a rental because of their one-day viewing promise. But with that off the table, it meant I needed more time to do viewings spread out on different days with different agents, and more time off work. I spent hours on the phone and online with different letting agents trying to find the perfect ground floor, garden flat for MJ, Sutro and I.

Everything was either too far to commute or too overpriced. I felt lost, overwhelmed and confused. I needed help.

The next day, when I officially started work, I met the man who hired me; AW, head of research and development. He was the most chilled-out business leader I've ever come across. It was a beautiful, sunny day in London and AW taught me that when that happens, the team goes to the pub across the road from the office for lunch. I said I needed to sort out my lost baggage dilemma and still find a place to live. He said as soon as I made those calls I should join them at the pub. I said okay.

"Hey if you don't find a place, you can move into the office until you get paid." AW joked.

If only that were a real option, I thought.

The calls were starting to seem hopeless. The properties I called about were either not on the market any more or the landlords didn't allow pets. The landlords who allowed pets were few and far between and they wanted a bigger security deposit too, which I didn't have. I was naive to think that I would get accommodation sorted in three days. I was also naive to think that I would get a ground-floor garden flat with my budget of £1,000 per month. We could hardly get a studio. But we needed a garden for Sutro. At night I called MJ and told him about the dilemma I was facing on the other side of the world. I'm not going to make it, I kept saying. I'm going to end up like one of those homeless people on the street. We spoke about maybe getting a smaller flat, a studio apartment for a month or two, then looking to get a bigger place afterwards when we'd both settled and MJ would have started working as well. Meanwhile, I was burning money at the AirBnB.

That evening I slept like a log. All the overwhelm and anxiety of the day disappeared as I closed my eyes. I hoped that tomorrow would be more promising in terms of getting more settled. I was excited to start our new lives in London.

On day 3 I still didn't find a permanent place to live. It made me anxious and everyone back at home in South Africa even more anxious, knowing I was in a strange place without any place to sleep. My mum knew someone who had their entire family living in London. The family offered, no, insisted that I come and stay with them until I found something permanent. I stayed there for a few days, but I was clearly encroaching on their lives. They had to rearrange their entire house in order to accommodate me, which they didn't mind at all, they were beyond hospitable. But I couldn't stay longer. I felt too much in the way.

That first night, I slept on a mattress in the kids room of the family friends of my mums. Through the bare window I could see the lights of West Ham Stadium glimmering in the distance. I was in the far east of London. The Green Street Hooligans part of London. I had no business there. So with nothing to lose, I posted a call out on Facebook. "Anyone in London, I need a place to stay for 4 days. Anyone, please?" If no one responded, I didn't know what I'd do. I was running out of options and money.

I woke up to the sounds of children running up and down

the stairs. They were getting the children ready for school. Still half asleep, I stared out the window. I remembered my Facebook post from the previous night and decided to open my phone. And there it was, the comment that changed the course of my life for the next few days.

```
Hey Leilah. Good to see you have moved to London
I am actually in Kuala Lumpur for another week so
my flat in Wapping is empty for the next 4 days.
Let me know if you're interested?
```

We met Chris the year before on our trip to Vietnam with Contiki. For ten days, we travelled together, from the north to the south of Vietnam, exploring the streets of Saigon, eating Bun bo Hue on the sidewalks of Hoi An, watching the festival of lights on the banks of Hue and dancing to Avicii on a junk boat in the middle of Halong Bay. Well, I didn't dance, obviously, but you get the picture. Still, Chris didn't really know us, know me, from a bar of soap. I could've been a dodgy South African Coloured, and here he was, opening up his home to me. It was a gesture that I knew I could never repay him for.

I ended up staying at Chris's flat for a week; longer than the original 4 days he offered. I didn't have an address yet, so I used his address to register my bills, without asking him first. I didn't think anything would ever be delivered there when I left, but weeks later Chris messaged me to say that I had mail delivered to his house. He even posted it to my new address, and I never offered to repay him. I overstayed my welcome, abused his kindness and made a total nuisance of myself. I was embarrassed for how I behaved, having my bills sent to his house. I took without giving back, which is out of character for me. But still, he brushed it off as nothing. He was a good friend. And I was too wrapped up in my own chaos to recognise it. Chris if you ever read this, know that you have been the lifesaver I needed and I am eternally grateful for you, for this gesture.

Eventually, I found a flat. It was a temporary rental. We called it our matchbox apartment. You could be on the bed, cook a meal and have one foot in the bathroom all at the same time. That's how small it was. The apartment was on the top floor of a beautiful Victorian building in a cul de sac in Clanricarde Gardens, Notting Hill. Down the street we had Portobello Market and across the road we had Hyde Park. I loved having a W2 postcode. We were living in one of the richest neighbourhoods in London, but we didn't have money for anything. MJ discovered that after 7pm every evening, the supermarkets would mark down all their meal deals to a fraction of the price in order to get them off the shelves, avoid food waster and make space for a fresh batch the next day. This meant we were able to buy sandwiches and wraps for something like 30p a pop. It kept us going for a while. We eventually also sold our wedding bands to get more cash for food and everyday things.

"We can always get it back," MJ said, as I slid the white gold ring with the tanzanite stone off my finger.

"Don't worry about it, I don't really care about the ring. We know we're married," I smiled back.

When the season changed, we tried on second-hand coats at the vintage stores in Notting Hill. For £5 each we were able to get a new wardrobe that was more appropriate attire for the harsh incoming Winter.

I thought of my dad less and less while in London. It was painful living in a place that reminded me every day that my dad had died. Being away from Cape Town, from everything that reminded me of him, from everyone that brought up his name in my presence, was liberating. It gave me time to process his death, it gave me the space and privacy to grieve. I felt that people expected me not to be sad about his death, for reasons not worth sharing, and that made me internalise a lot of my grief. After all, I was a pro at zombifying myself.

For my mum, seeing me being able to broaden my career in London was the pinnacle of achievement for her. All her efforts materialised. It meant she could finally take a break because all her hard work was all worth it. She struggled to put me through school and college mostly by herself. She put herself through a mountain of debt and it was extremely difficult for her. But she wanted me to complete my studies, so I could have a better life with better opportunities. Better than the ones she was given as a teenager finishing school in the apartheid era.

You'll never see it all

Three months later, we moved out of Notting Hill and into Sydenham, South East London to a ground floor garden flat. And only then was Sutro able to join us. MJ went to fetch her on a British Airways Boeing. With the three of us finally together again, that's when we could start acclimatising to our new home. MJ got a job as a data scientist at a luxury beauty brand. He hated it, and soon found something else at a different company. I kept reminding him that he didn't need to stick to one career field.

"You can be anything you want in London. You can start over, do what you really want to do. So go on, be anything you want." I said.

I had started to settle into my new role at work and everyone in my team were great to work with. I came into the team with this legacy of having won 12 awards for the automobile brand, one of them that made global agency news, so that helped. Everyone had already known who I was (and thought I was shit hot at creative work). Imposter syndrome was still a friend, but I saw her less and less.

We walked Sutro at one of the two parks down the street from our flat. Getting to work required three tube changes, which made the commute even longer. We left Sutro alone in the garden while we were at work. We knew Sydenham was not a long-term solution either, but it was fine for the moment.

"There's so much to do and see in London, and you'll never see it all," an Uber driver told me.

I was starting to see what he meant. When I recall my first few days starting a new job in a new country, I remember feeling a similar sort of way. Walking into the towers of the Iridium London office for the first time I felt uncomfortable. Almost invisible. The office was made up of two floors, with roughly 700 desks, a much larger scale of Iridium than the Cape Town office. It was larger in the same way that everything in London was larger than life to me. The streets were busier, the shops were plentiful, you were never too far away from a Pret a Manger. In Cape Town only a few stores were experimenting with online shopping, but in London online shopping, contactless payment and self-checkout was the standard. All our favourite bands played sold-out stadiums every weekend in London. Events were happening everywhere, concept pop-ups existed on every street corner, everything was 10x. I felt out of place because I was not used to this heightened level of everything. Overstimulated. Coming from a small beach town in South Africa, London was a sensory overload.

The creative team at work were about 12 people, including me. I was one of two Content Directors in the team and I joined more or less the same time as my new manager, Pete.

"We're trying to shift the way the agency is perceived in the rest of the network. We want to be seen as more creative, while still focusing on performance. And that's why you and Pete are here. We want you two to drive innovation across the agency," AW told me.

Pete was a manager like no other. He challenged my belief of what I thought managers were like. He was different. He was supportive. He listened. He cared about making great work that meant something. He didn't only care about the money — he would never let that cloud a brief or a creative decision. He taught me how to stand up for our creative values, showed me that I had a voice and how to use it to my advantage. He single-handedly restored my confidence after years and years of it being broken down, working in stressed-out conditions under bad managers. I soon learned that working in this team was less about the marketing science and more about the art of creative production. And I revelled in it. I loved having a purpose and knowing exactly why I was brought into the team. It made me feel needed. Valued. And closer to ad land than ever before. Here, I was truly making ads. Finally. Digital ads, but they were ads. *I had made it*, I thought.

For six glorious months, we made epic creative work. We made work we believed in for some of Britain's biggest and most well-known brands. Account directors would come to us with a seedling of a creative brief. The two of us would interrogate it, he'd let me run ideation sessions with the rest of the team and come back to him with a few solid creative ideas. I was putting slide decks together in 30 mins — I became that good at delivering a creative pitch.

"Interrogate the brief," he'd say. "If we get crisp on the problem and the insight, we'll create better work." He was right.

We'd win pitches and take work from traditional creative agencies. This was it. This was that thing I was chasing for such a long time. The opportunity to see my work out there, an idea that came from my brain, brought to life as an ad for a brand. I was living the dream I was chasing, right here in London. We made waves throughout the agency. Directors in this 700-person agency knew me by name and it was all thanks to Pete. He made sure that my work was recognised not only at his level, but at the highest level of the agency. He set me up for the biggest promotion of my career: Creative Director, London. There was nothing I wanted more in life than to have that title, but I thought that would only come years later. I was beyond chuffed.

And then the news dropped. Pete got an offer to transfer to our New York office. I was gutted. When Pete left, the agency went through a bunch of changes. We restructured, the leadership team changed and the experimental creative team that lived inside an agency with a performance DNA, was no longer a priority. Content marketing was a long bet for the agency. It didn't quite equal *money maker.* If we had more time, maybe we could prove that it could be a money maker. I was able to provide proof of concept for the department I started in Cape Town, so I was sure we would be able to do the same here. But we didn't have time on our side. The restructure was brutal. Half of my team were redeployed to product teams that needed their skills more and they had to pivot from being creative content producers to something else. Pete's replacement started soon after he left. And that's all I will say about him.

My mum came to visit us after we settled into our new home. We showed her all our favourite local spots and also all the must-see tourist attractions. We went shopping in Oxford Street, people watching at Trafalgar Square, we saw the changing of the guards at Westminster Abbey, and listened to the debates at Speakers' Corner in Hyde Park. We also did a mini food tour on Brick Lane and Borough Market. For as long as I can remember, my mum has been dreaming of travelling, of seeing the world. When I was a teenager, she told me about the turquoise water on white sandy beaches that she would love to see, and the exotic places that she longed to visit. My mum and her sisters grew up travelling around Africa. My grandfather took them on trips every summer, exploring a different part of the continent, like Mozambique or Swaziland. Before he got cancer, he was finalising preparations for them to emigrate to Rio de Janeiro in Brazil. But then he passed away in Cape Town, and they never left. Their lives also changed dramatically.

My mum would've had a very different life had they still moved, and I wouldn't be here right now. My grandfather introduced my mum to travel; she fell in love with the idea of seeing other places, seeing the rest of the world. But travelling from South Africa has never been easy for us. Though travel wasn't specifically banned for people of colour during the apartheid era, it was near impossible for us to travel. It was a luxury that many people of colour couldn't afford as they were forced into menial jobs where they were exploited and underpaid. For years my mum believed that she'd never be able to leave Cape Town again, to see the rest of the world.

Our move to London also blessed me with the opportunity to give my mum the gift of travelling. Now she had a passport and collected stamps in every city she passed through on her way to London to visit us. It was a satisfying bonus that came with the privilege of being an immigrant in one of the greatest cities in the world.

* * *

When Pete left, the creative team took a dive in the wrong direction. The type of briefs we got were different. The work we produced was different. The energy in the team was so different. And maybe I could've done more to improve the culture in the team, being the Creative Director and all that, but I too, became indifferent. I was dealing with orienting myself after a series of significant changes in a short space of time. I knew I needed to be present, working, but it was hard trying to recover from the aftermath of the restructure, and also losing the support of Pete.

There were days, months, where I felt that I didn't want to carry on any more. I did the thing I always do when I'm trying to cope with a difficult situation; I retreated. What grounded me was the thought that everything in life was temporary. A reminder to accept the bad times and enjoy the good times to the fullest because they won't last forever. I knew that this too, shall pass. Iridium tried to bolster our content team by unofficially merging it with an existing content team from one of our established content agencies in the network. They placed a small team of content specialists in our office, so we'd operate as one team. Two senior writers and two account directors. They moved into the empty bank of desks next to mine and seemed cheerful, approachable. I should go over and introduce myself, I thought. But I didn't.

A few hours later, one of the girls walked over to my desk.

"Hey, I'm Liz," she smiled.

"I'm Leilah, it's nice to meet you."

She was one of the writers at the agency. We talked about what we were working on, what kind of coffee we liked and then she introduced me to the rest of her team. I watched her move around between desks, saying hello to every person in the team, politely shaking everyone's hands. She made conversations seem so effortless. Liz was one of those people who had a magnetic energy about them, the kind who could light up a room just with their presence. I instantly gravitated towards her.

We didn't work on many projects together, as Liz focused on editorial and my projects were all for social media, but we did find many opportunities to brainstorm ideas together. I valued Liz's opinions on ideas; she brought a fresh perspective to the team that was very much needed. And I enjoyed being around her as her aura lifted me up, so I would seek her out everyday for coffee and conversations. I hope I gave her something in return for the good vibes she gave me, because she never once complained or called me annoying.

Where are your creative values?

So the promotion to Creative Director didn't officially materialise until after Pete left. We were talking about it, but with the uncertainty of the restructure and the merger with the new agency, I didn't know if it would still go ahead. So it was a shock when I got the letter handed to me by the head of the agency. The first person I told, apart from MJ, my family, and Liz, was Pete. We still kept in touch after he left.

```
WOO! You'll have to work on the bits of your game
that you know you have to work on.
You've been promoted, which is the agency's way of
saying... 'we think you're really fucking good'...
So now you don't have to worry about that side of
things.

You have to remember to stand for something. You're
there to be the creative heartbeat of the agency,
you're there to make sure the work is as good as it
can be and you're there to inject energy into those
around you.

I think you'll grow into the role and I think you'll
```

```
have 20 new awards, but for London this time!

Embrace it and remember, no one ever feels like
they're ready to take the jump... and if you feel
ready, you've procrastinated too much.

OWN IT. You'll be brilliant!
```

Emailing Pete about the aftermath of the restructure, the new challenges I was facing at the agency was very helpful. It made me see things through a different lens and kept me inspired when I felt like there was nothing to bet on. I was worried about losing my job and my visa, and that took a lot of energy from me. I just wanted to stop worrying about visa issues and just focus on making great work. But our department went from experimental to volatile and unless I was bringing in million dollar client accounts everyday, there was no job security. Everyone was at risk. A very weird way to operate a creative team. If you're on a skilled worker visa, you're not allowed to work for any other company other than the one that's sponsoring your visa. If I did decide that I wanted to change jobs, then I'd have to go through the same process again. The company has to prove that they can't find the talent in the country and therefore want to sponsor me. It doesn't matter if I'm already in the country because at the end of the day, I was still a migrant.

Only once you've lived in the country for five years under a skilled worker visa, you can apply for Indefinite Leave to Remain - which is permanent residency or settlement status.

This means that the company you're employed at, or any company for that matter, doesn't have to sponsor you any more and you no longer need a visa to live and work in the United Kingdom. This was my end goal. To be able to choose which company I wanted to work at, and not needing a visa to work. Heck I could even choose to not work full time if I wanted to. Just the opportunity to be able to choose. To be on the same level playing field as British citizens. Freedom. That was my end goal for sure.

* * *

I was in year three of my five-year sentence. My visa was also expiring soon, and I needed to get the agency to renew my visa so that MJ, Sutro and I could stay in the country. This unique position created an internal battle for me; to either push for greater quality work which meant taking a risk, standing up and fighting for my creative values, as Pete taught me, or go with the flow and be a people-pleaser. Pete taught me that I could disagree with clients, that they paid us because we're the experts and they want us to do our best with their account even if it meant disagreeing with their approach. The right client will take the risk with you, and reap the rewards with you. But the agency didn't understand that. They wanted the money, and to them that meant agreeing with everything the client wanted. Being a yes-woman. With Pete, AW and most of the leadership team I once knew gone, I didn't know what the new leadership at Iridium wanted from me. What type of Creative Director did they want? I definitely wanted to be the one they wanted so that I could keep my visa and continue my life in London. I didn't want to create a fuss and be let go.

Pete and I spoke about this often.

> I feel your pain. The tough thing is you think
> you're going crazy... and that maybe you have the
> problem. But just to let you know, it's not you. In
> the right environment, passion for the work is
> saluted. If someone loses their shit here because
> the idea is being killed, it's fine because it's
> about doing the best for your client.
>
> You'll get there! And, at the very worst, you'll
> come out of this with a brilliant portfolio of work!
> Clients pay you to challenge them. If they didn't
> want a challenge, they'd just use you as an
> execution agency!
>
> Work with no fire behind it isn't work. It's a
> process.
>
> Trouble is, when you work in an environment that
> constantly asks you to drop your creative integrity,
> it's hard to get that consistency. It's what makes
> the industry so garbage in the main

I wrote back:

> Everyday is the same repetition - I can't honestly
> say I'm doing mind-blowing work. I haven't had
> client communication in months. I haven't presented
> anything in months. I've not been challenged in any
> shape or form, probably since you were here.
>
> And it's made me softer. And I know what you're
> thinking; I shouldn't rely on other people for my
> own growth.. But I haven't. I've stepped up and put

> myself out there, for pitches, for more
> responsibility, I wrote creative values for the
> team, pitched hack programmes, you name it.. But I'm
> told to shut it down. And somewhere along the line I
> just stopped caring.
>
> I don't want to be seen as soft.

And he'd write back:

> I think the mediocrity thing only happens if you
> allow it to. If people around you are creating
> average work, you have to reject it. You also have
> to encourage people to believe that every piece of
> work that goes out is a reflection of the agency...
> and an open door of opportunity if you get it right.
> I think you'll only blend in if you let it happen,
> which I know you won't!
>
> I think reading great books and going to events is a
> good way to keep yourself sharp!
> I think you need someone more creatively mature to
> partner with, that'll massively help. Coming up with
> ideas on your own is tough. I'm not sure the support
> you have at the moment is good enough.

At the same time, I also applied for jobs externally. I decided to take matters into my own hands and instead of waiting to see whether the agency would extend my visa, I had to start doing something to secure my future in London. But it was a harder pitch. As soon as the outside world learnt that I needed a visa, that they would need to sponsor me, the conversations would be cut short. One agency told me off for not being upfront with them. They said if they knew I needed a visa they wouldn't have bothered speaking to me in the first place. The pool of agencies to contact had become smaller and smaller. Pete thought I should aim higher.

```
I think you're ready to take on something way better
than you're aiming for. Careers are short, be at the
best, most creative place you can find... you'll be
inspired, working amongst your own and fighting for
better, not average.

P.
```

I went to so many different interviews that year. Big companies, small companies, brands, agencies, publishing houses, tech companies, gaming companies, retail companies, you name it. Everyone had the same response: no visa, no job, sorreeeeeeee.

I was an introverted mixed-race female trying to be seen in a world of ballsy White men in suits speaking over each other in the boardroom. It was starting to feel like a lost cause. I was drained, mentally and physically, and interviewers could smell it.

I told Liz that I was interviewing outside of the agency. We've become close over the months since our teams merged. She was the only person at the agency who saw the real me, who got me. She made me feel human. But the agency wasn't offering her any reason to stay either, and soon she got a better offer and left. But we still met up occasionally on the weekend for brunch, or after work for Thai food. We'd pick the place we both loved on Charlotte Street down the road from Iridium in central London.

Liz also always brought a gift to our meets; a notebook with a quote that made her think of me, new pens because I loved stationery, luxury hand cream that I would never buy myself because I thought it too expensive. We'd spend hours catching up, I'd fill her in on the latest drama at the office. She'd encourage me to go to the team social events, to get involved in activities so that I wouldn't feel so alone at work. She wanted me to feel included in things, even without her there.

When we left the restaurant, we'd always make plans for the next meet up. Liz made sure to get a date booked in the diary. And I'd watch her stroll away in her cool boxy coat, blonde hair tucked into her collar and an oversized scarf wrapped snug around her neck, excitedly waiting for the next time I'd see her again.

You won't fit in with the culture

~2018~

In my fourth year of holding a skilled worker visa at Iridium, and 1 year left till I got Indefinite Leave to Remain, they decided not to renew my visa. Instead, they gave me a different sort of gift: redundancy. The agency had changed their leadership team one more time and the new leader wanted to shift things around too. This meant that people were shifted around too. Except me. They couldn't find a transferable role for a Creative Director within a performance agency. So I was made redundant. It was disheartening because that year I was finally growing into my role as a Creative Director, finding my voice. For the longest time it has been my dream to hold the Creative Director title. I didn't think I could do it, because traditionally, Creative Directors have loud, obnoxious, god-like presences. They demand respect when they walk into a room. I didn't possess such a quality. But I've done a lot of work on finding my true self, my true voice that year and it was more along the lines of an alpha wolf in the wild. When studying wolves, Carl Safina notes that an alpha isn't one who leads with loud bravado or bared teeth. The defining trait of an alpha wolf is a quiet confidence and self-assurance. They know what they need to do and what's best for the pack, and they carry that certainty with a calming presence. And when the situation called for it, the alpha can assert themselves decisively. I was a total alpha wolf that year.

The redundancy came as a shock to me. A week before, I had just won another pitch for a social client. It was small, but it was still money. I got back from lunch one day and my sixth new manager that year stood with our HR director and asked if I had a minute to 'quickly chat' with them.

"Sure," I said. I thought it was about my visa. I had never spoken to HR about anything else before ever in the four years of working at the agency.

"Your role is at risk of redundancy," my manager said very matter-of-factly.

She went on to explain the redundancy process, what I should expect to happen next and what my options were. My options were none. Outside of the agency, I needed a visa to get a new job. And inside the agency, I needed a job to have my visa extended. I was screwed either way. Iridium had the duty to let the government know that I was no longer an employee so that they could proceed with having my visa revoked. They gave me three month's notice as per my contract. Three months to find another job and another company to sponsor my visa. MJ didn't need a sponsorship, as he had a spousal visa. But his visa was dependent on my sponsorship. If mine was revoked, so was his.

I sat silently watching this woman dictate the terms of my life to me. Making the call of whether I got to stay in the country. I understood it was all business, but after everything I'd given this company, all of my best years devoted to this company, I felt let down. The birth of content marketing, scaling it across countries, the extra revenue stream, all the pitches won, remaining at peak performance despite all the changes they threw at me. I felt let down in the worst way. My manager didn't think it was a big deal; she asked why I didn't want to go back to South Africa. MJ, Sutro and I had been living in the country for four years already at the time. London was our life. London was home. We weren't prepared to leave. Especially not on someone else's terms. But I was a second-rate citizen. A beggar for an opportunity to stay.

That evening I was too drained to take the tube home so I ordered an Uber. On the day where I just felt like crawling into a ball inside myself, I got a chatty driver. We talked about where we're both from; he was from Ghana. He asked me if I'd like to stay in the country and I said yeah if the government allowed me to, and he said, "you know what, if it's in your heart and your intentions are pure, then you will stay." I was desperate to believe him.

Iridium committed to finding me a suitable role within one of the sister agencies in the network. It seemed promising. I continued to interview outside the network as a plan B, but as before, interviews never led to anything because I needed a visa. The interviews were also much harder this time, naturally. Because when you're interviewing for a job, as well as interviewing for your life in the UK, there's a lot more at stake. It took everything to not let companies see the desperation in my eyes. It only worked half the time. Needless to say, landing another job internally within the network seemed like a more promising route. I wouldn't need to change my visa, it would just naturally be extended because I'd still be employed by the parent company. So I focused on wowing the agencies in our network, setting up coffee meet-ups with creative leaders, hoping a job would materialise from those meets. It never did.

* * *

Because of my tenure at the agency, Iridium was required to give me three months' notice if they wanted to terminate my contract. This was the limbo period during which I had to find another job, essentially another visa sponsor, so that we could stay in the UK. Iridium was my longest working stint. I saw so many people who were there before me, like Pete and AW, leave the agency and move on. AW, I do hope you're in a better place now and that you're resting in peace.

So I was told by HR that I had some options. Lucky me. Option one was I could choose to either continue working for the agency for the next three months as usual. As if. Option two was I could go on gardening leave where I'd be at home but would not have access to my laptop or work email. I can't remember what option three was, because I had already decided to take option two. The risk of redundancy dangled on whether I would be able to get another role within the business, the wider network of 12 other agencies, all of whom sold content of some sort as a service. If I lost access to my work laptop and email account, I would automatically lose access to that network. I was pretty confident I'd find something in the network within the next three months. I mean, 12 digital marketing and creative agencies within the network. One of them would be bound to have a role for an award-winning Creative Director, right? I chose to wrap up my existing projects and then go on gardening leave.

Before going on gardening leave, I met almost every hiring manager at every agency within our network. Not once, not twice. Three times, four times, sometimes with presentations attached to my fourth meeting. I had the most important deadline of my life. If I couldn't charm these people in the next three months to hire me or re-hire me, then MJ, Sutro and I would be on a flight to Cape Town. A flight we couldn't even afford. I didn't even want to think about how we would transport Sutro back to Cape Town. She'd spent more years in London than in Cape Town. She was a proper Londoner already.

Before I went on gardening leave, I asked for a meeting with the Managing Director. Stellar guy. He'd just come back from a few years in our United States office and was appointed as the London agency's Chief Strategy Officer. Soon after he was promoted to Managing Director. It was a smart move for the agency; Jack understood the importance of creativity in a performance marketing industry. He was also a genuinely nice guy. In our last company-wide social, we landed up in the same team. He aptly named our team the Punks and that spoke to my soul, naturally. By then the only sign of punk I carried with me were the two silver studs in my lip and my purple hair.

I still listened to punk music occasionally, but my wardrobe started to blend from leather armbands and ripped jeans to a somewhat corporate London look.

"Leilah, I'm so sorry this is happening to you. How can I help make this easier for you?" Jack asked after I told him about my situation.

"I need to find a job in the network to keep my visa and stay in the UK," I said. I explained that under the Tier 2 visa system, a company had to sponsor me for a specific role. That sponsorship allowed me to live and work in the country. Without a confirmed job from an approved UK employer, I would lose my visa and face deportation.

"So you can't stay in the country if you lose the work visa?" He asked.

"No."

"Hmm. Okay, well let's not panic yet. We have some time, right? How long do you have until..." he didn't finish his sentence, but we both knew what he meant. Until I had to leave the country. Until I was kicked out. Until I was deported. Until my entire life in the UK would be uprooted and destroyed.

"Just under three months now. It's not long, if you think about the recruitment process." I clarified.

"So tell me who you have spoken to already, and then let me reach out to the rest of the agencies in the group. Between us,

I'm sure we can find you something," he said confidently.

His confidence in this approach reassured me for a while. If anyone had influence in the network, it was Jack. And with his endorsement, I would surely be able to get a foot in the door somewhere. I would keep my visa. I was hopeful.

Days later Jack came by my desk and sat in the empty chair next to me.

"Good news," he said.

"Oh yeah?"

"Yeah. So I've spoken to Beowulf and Film Nexus about you and there seems to be a role going at both. You'd be a shoe in for both."

He went on to explain the two roles in detail, telling me how my skills could be transferred and the strengths I could bring to those agencies. He really knew me. He knew about the work I had done for the agency, he knew what I was passionate about, my creative values, my strengths. As well as that, it sounded like he believed in me. His words were genuine.

"So go hard at both, and then you'll have options. Okay?" He finished.

I nodded and smiled trying to blink away tears. "Thank you so much. You have no idea how much this means to me."

"Don't worry about it. Please come back and tell me how both interviews went. Promise?" He said before getting up and moving to his next meeting.

Finally. Someone was showing up for me. And the head of the agency, no less. He didn't have to. It wasn't his job to find me a replacement role. It was my manager and HR's job to do that. Just two weeks ago I emailed my manager to let her know that I was disappointed that I wasn't getting the support she promised when I volunteered to wrap up my ongoing projects before taking gardening leave. The support was basic, an update on planned headcount in the network, continued one to one meetings with my manager, at the very least, a check-in on how I was doing while job-searching and planning my potential move back to South Africa. But instead I got nothing. No communication, my one-to-one meetings with my manager were cancelled. She went on holiday and asked our HR department to finalise my redundancy consultation and paperwork before she came back, so she wouldn't have to deal with it after her holiday. Like I was an annoying piece of admin that inconvenienced her life. Her cushy little life in the British countryside, where she could return to with her husband and children every day after work and not have to worry about immigration issues. Unfortunately, I didn't have that luxury.

I went to Film Nexus first. The guy I met was friendly and welcoming and obviously very proud of where he worked. He took me on a tour throughout the office and introduced me to most of the people we passed along the way. He showed me where they made ads, the studio where they filmed everything and I think my heart skipped a beat. After the tour, we entered a small, cubicle-style meeting room where he had my CV printed in front of him. He kept looking at it and asked me pointed questions which I appreciated. I studied these specific questions before the interview. He nodded as I spoke, asked me follow-up questions and complimented me on the parts of my story where I described some of the work I'd done. It was going well.

"Thanks so much for coming in, it was a real pleasure to meet you Leilah." He said as we parted ways. "I'll be in touch."

He was in touch. The very next day, he emailed to let me know that they had decided to put the role on hold as their budget for the year was locked. But if I got in touch next year, they would be happy to offer me the position without having to interview again.

"Thank you," I responded, without any detail of why that wouldn't be an option for me. I didn't have a whole year. I had less than two months and counting. And I needed to land something now, or face moving my whole life back to South Africa.

The next interview was at Beowulf. They were the last agency acquired by the network in the UK and therefore were not based in our towers. They were based in the next road in a very vibrant part of London, the Heals building. Entering the building, I was already impressed. I entered the glass elevators to the 6th floor. The elevator opened directly in their offices. I stood in the open plan space, looking for a reception desk. People had their heads down working in isolation on their computers; a contrast to the vibrancy outside of the building. There was no reception area. I looked around, looked for someone, anyone to let them know that I had arrived for my interview. A tall, lanky man with shaggy hair emerged from behind a desk. He was the Executive Creative Director and he said he would be conducting the interview. The position was for a Creative Strategist; a Content Strategist. Easy, I thought. That's exactly what I do. The first thing he told me was that he couldn't print my CV, because of something with the printer. Apparently he tried to print it in several different ways, but it wouldn't print. He also didn't want me to talk him through my CV. He said he'd read it over after the interview. Fine, I thought. This is fine.

It wasn't fine. We started with small talk and at the right moment, I whipped out my latest piece of branded content work I'd conceptualised, wrote, art directed and oversaw to production. It was a comic book for a British energy services giant. He asked me two or three questions about my career and decided that he wasn't going to hire me.

"Your work is great, but I just don't think that you'll fit in here with the culture," he said.

I smiled and nodded, the look of defeat crystal clear on my face.

"I'm sorry. I know that's not what you wanted to hear, but it's a really important role and we have to get it right," he explained.

I don't fit in with the culture? What did that even mean? I could've probed. I could've asked him to explain himself. But it felt like he had already made the decision before even speaking to me. It was the shortest interview I ever had. I had given it my all. I answered his plain questions thoughtfully and meaningfully, selling myself hard but in my quietly confident way. Was that it? Was my quietness counting against me? I obsessed about that one line for days after the interview. *You won't fit in with the culture.*

Assessing a candidate for a cultural fit, I learned, is based on a soft skills assessment. It's deciding whether someone would be able to adapt to the core values and behaviour that make up a business. I had been working in the same network for over five years at the time, so I could recite the core values off by heart and backwards if I wanted to. However, there are other more tangible questions you can ask a candidate to get a better understanding of them and therefore make a judgement call on whether they are a good culture fit. Questions such as having them describe their ideal work environment, how they deal with pressure, what they need to be productive, their dream job, passions, favourite book, ideal work schedule, etc. Corporations who are serious about culture fit will ask candidates to do a personality quiz beforehand as part of the initial screening. But this was nothing like that. I don't think he learned anything about me in the interview. He couldn't have because he didn't ask me any culture-fit questions. There was nothing I could do to come back from feedback like that, and so I gathered my bag and blazer and saw myself out.

After the interview I stood on the pavement of the busy, bustling London street and called MJ.

"How did it go?" He said as soon as he answered the call.

"They said I won't fit in with their culture." I cried. I cried and cried in the middle of the street in front of the agency's building, not caring who saw me at that moment. I had hit rock bottom.

On my last day before heading off on gardening leave, I erased my personal information from my laptop and shut it down for the final time before handing it back to the agency. I placed it on my manager's desk, along with my work phone, ID badge and a note that read *Leilah's things*. I said goodbye to the few people who knew what was going on and made my way out the building.

"Make sure you email all your contacts in the network and give them your personal email address so that they can contact you if anything pops up," Someone told me.

"And keep in touch!"

Nothing is guaranteed, not even tomorrow

While on gardening leave, my mum was staying with us. She came over at least once a year for a holiday and spent an average of three months with us. When she visited, we'd have three months of MJ's favourite home-cooked meals, and three months of me being a bum on the sofa. Even though I was going through hell trying to land a job with a visa, I also appreciated the extra time off work that I could spend with my mum. Between interviews, we'd take Sutro for a walk and sit on the park benches for hours, just staring into the distance. Neither of us speaking a word, silently stressing about the future. When I tried to speak, I cried. That became our sad new routine for a while.

I continued to apply for new content roles that were advertised in the network. I even applied to the non-content roles. I applied externally as well. It felt like everything was working against me. I was competing for jobs with people who didn't need visas. It wasn't a fair match.

In one interview for a tech startup, I sat in a boardroom with the CEO and CSO (too many O's) presenting my past work banging on about all my awards. Gold for this category, gold for that category and this one was best in class. I could tell that none of this mattered to a company like theirs. This was a tech startup, focusing on health and wellness through the lens of serious chronic conditions. This wasn't Mercedes-Benz, British Gas or The Body Shop. My accomplishments in the creative industry clearly meant nothing at this company. Still, I continued my presentation, it was like I couldn't read the room.

The CEO stopped me and asked, "Why do you want to work for a company like ours?"

I think he was genuinely confused about what I was doing in their meeting room, pitching myself, when I had this roster of awards on my belt and famous brands I'd worked for. And here I was sitting at their health-tech startup, with a small team, no creative department, no budget and that was on nobody's radar. Yet. What they did have was a licence to sponsor immigrant workers. And you know, beggars can't be choosers, so there I was.

I thought about my answer carefully. "I've been in the ad agency business for 10 years. I'm always jumping between projects because of the nature of our work. Sometimes we get to do the full pitch but we don't always land the account, so I never get to see my ideas through to execution. I'd like to move to a company where I can focus on the in-house brand wholeheartedly. At this point in my life, I also want to work on something that's more closely aligned with my personal values. I want to do something meaningful with my career," I said.

None of that was a lie. But I'd be lying if I said I hadn't rehearsed that line specifically for a cruelty-free beauty brand instead.

I had spent 10 years in the agency business getting pumped about brands that walk in and out of my life in the space of three weeks. I'd get totally invested in a brand and pour my heart and soul out into the pitch only to have them say they didn't have the budget for creative services right now. I also heard from my friends on the other side that pitching was a brand's way of generating fresh ideas for free. So some brands would go into the pitch process without the intention of ever hiring an agency. And I was genuinely sick of that.

I left the startup's tiny office and made my way back to Farringdon tube station. I was already so used to rejection that I wasn't even sad about it any more. When I got home, I got a call from one of the O's. I got the job! This is when I dropped the visa bomb. I knew the spiel already. I got loads of 'you got the job' calls before, and when I dropped the visa bomb, I told them I needed a visa to start working for them, they retracted the offer. This is what I was waiting for from the tech startup. But something else happened instead.

They didn't bat an eyelid at having to sponsor my visa because half the staff were expats, so it was something they were quite used to doing as a company. I couldn't believe my eyes and ears as the news came in writing and on the phone. Our tiny household in Clarendon Road, London cried a massive sigh of relief that day. And only then did I realise the immense amount of anxiety that MJ and my mum were experiencing behind the scenes of my turmoil. I didn't quite realise the toll my stress took on them at the time. At night after supper, I'd hear them whispering in the garden, but I was too busy trying to escape in the latest episode of something on Netflix. They tried to explore every single angle to help me, but they were helpless. There was nothing they could do, and that devastated them both. When I got the confirmation that my visa was extended, or transferred, with the tech startup being my new sponsor, we celebrated quietly with a Deliveroo takeaway, followed by all the junk food and snacks afterwards. We ate our feelings.

When the paperwork was finalised and I held my new Biometric Residence Card in my hands, everyone exhaled. My mum had extended her flight so many times because she thought she'd have to help us move back to Cape Town. This news meant she was also able to exhale, and return to her life in Cape Town, to my family that were also anxiously waiting to hear the news.

"I'll see you soon again, mum. Thank you for everything," I said as we hugged at the airport.

MJ and I watched as my mum made her way through airport security and then disappeared behind the duty-free shopping centre. She was on her way back to Cape Town from an extended and stressful holiday with us. We were on our way back to South West London to walk Sutro in our local park down the street from our home. The home that we still got to keep, thanks to a wild miracle and alignment of stars in our destiny. It was a bold lesson that made me remember something very fundamental about life. Nothing is guaranteed. Not even tomorrow.

A new job and Obsessive Compulsive Disorder

On my first day as head of marketing at the startup, I cried at my desk. I cried for the opportunities I could've had if only I didn't need a visa. I cried for all the job offers I got before this one, at pedigree agencies, that were retracted because of visa issues. I cried for the years I spent yearning to be in a creative agency. I cried for broken dreams, disappointments and 548 days that I would need to wait in order to be truly free in Great Britain. But the voice in my head told me that crying is being ungrateful. So I flipped my perspective; I was healthy, my family was healthy, I had a partner who shared the same values as me, we had a dog we loved and we were granted another few years in London. That was happiness.

When I took my first class of creative writing at Varsity College back in 2005, I never knew that one day I would be writing about chronic health conditions. I'm sure my lecturers couldn't have predicted it either. They said they saw me at an Ad Makers, an FCB, an Ogilvy. Yet, here I was. On the one hand I was doing something meaningful with my time. I was raising awareness of online support groups for people living with chronic health conditions and long-term illness, such as cancer, heart disease, lupus, anxiety and depression etc. But on the other hand, I was so drastically far away from my dream that the dream was starting to fade. Cannes Lion, who?

But right now was not the time to mope, I decided. This company had given me extra time in the country. I was so close to the five-year mark when I could finally apply for permanent residency, and I couldn't mess it up. All I needed was this last one year and a half as a sponsored migrant under this skilled worker visa. And this company was prepared to do it for me. In return for my brilliance. My creative brilliance that I wasn't sure I possessed any more. Their office was tiny, very different to the global offices I was used to. I had a desk in the middle of the office against a brick wall. The laptop they gave me was old and used. But the commute was a dream. Thirty minutes on the northern line to Moorgate, a quick change to Farringdon, and there I was. I started to see the small glories in all of this. And the one very big obvious blessing of course; we got to stay in London. But the entire time I worked at the startup, I was insecure about losing my job and losing my visa. Because I'd been burned before, I thought it would happen again.

When I eventually settled into my role, I learnt more about myself than I'd ever done before. I also learnt that there was nothing that I couldn't achieve, if I set my mind to it. Ramping up was hard because the product was complex. To familiarise myself with the product and the industry, I created a multi-channel branded content strategy that was rooted in creativity. I showed the business that if we could communicate to people in their own language, with empathy and feeling, then we would raise awareness of the support groups faster. We couldn't do that with cold, hard statistics and facts about illnesses. And that was the single biggest contribution I made to the business, because it changed their entire approach to marketing going forward.

I filled my days activating that strategy, creating beautiful content, growing their social and digital channels, creating a blog with regular blog posts and sourcing ambassadors for guest content. I asked real people from the communities to share their stories; to share the human truth behind these health conditions. With their explicit permission, of course. I also influenced other parts of the startup's digital presence, like the corporate website that received a redesign, both in writing and information architecture, the brand logo, the product value propositioning and the email marketing strategy. I worked with research teams to surface important numbers and insights in things like whitepapers, webinars and other collateral. I used these as lead magnets on our website to grow our database. In between all of that, I figured out how to do PR for the startup as well, organising spots for the company at industry events and setting up guest speaking opportunities for our CEO. As head of marketing, all content production fell under my remit. And that meant I also had to create event materials like roller banners, leaflets, business cards and swag. I planned, storyboarded, filmed and edited video content for pitches and social content. I also created a brand style guide where I established tone of voice guidelines and treatment of the brand and logo on all channels.

"Can you write a speech for the CEO for this event next week?"

"Sure!"

"Shareholders report for our investors?"

"Why not!"

I soon became the go-to person for all things content and the final point of quality assessment for all external brand communications. I was doing the job of an entire marketing team and I enjoyed myself thoroughly. Even though the subject matter was mundane and depressing, the creative process was exciting. It was my first experience working in a startup, and I soon figured out that I could make my role whatever I wanted it to be. There were no set guidelines, just goals and how I got there was up to me. It was an environment that suited me well. I first discovered my entrepreneurial spirit when I created a social media department at Indigo Star. Then it surfaced again later at Iridium where I created the content marketing department and scaled it across countries. The years I spent at structured corporations, where I learnt how to break out of the box, had served me well in my role at the startup.

I worked with the friendliest people who welcomed me instantly. I loved being part of and shaping the culture of the business. Even if it was just organising forced fun activities for the rest of the team, like Halloween and holiday parties, movie nights at the office and scavenger hunts. For my first Halloween at the office I used my own money to buy Halloween props and headwear for people who conveniently forgot to come dressed up in costume. I didn't expense it back because submitting expenses was not a thing at the startup. But I didn't care. I cared about culture and the spirit of community, and I was invested in building and cultivating community spirit. It's what gave me purpose when I didn't really feel inspired by the product.

The work drained me in a way that I could not easily recover from. Everyday I learned about a new chronic health condition, the symptoms, the treatment and the daily struggle that people living with these conditions had to endure. Everyday my mental health took a turn for the worse. While my colleagues were able to forget about the vivid detail of living with a chronic condition as soon as they left the building, I was not. I found it extremely hard to let go of my work when my work day ended. As an empath, I absorbed the stories and energies of these anonymous posters. I experienced the horror through their words. I'd dream about it at night and I'd catastrophise thinking that I too would develop multiple chronic conditions. In a way, working with that subject matter, was incredibly unhealthy for me. I absorbed all the heaviness and carried it with me everyday. And Lord knows I didn't need any more heaviness in my life. It's also here, where I decided to diagnose myself with Obsessive Compulsive Disorder (OCD), because I recognised many of the symptoms in myself. There is no test to diagnose OCD. A healthcare specialist will make a diagnosis after asking you a series of questions about your symptoms. I had the call with a specialist, they asked me the same series of questions, and concluded that I might have OCD. Though my therapist now says that it's likely I don't have OCD, just a heightened level of anxiety. I knew that this job wasn't sustainable for me, but I also knew it was a means to an end, my permanent residency in the UK, and so I kept on and carried on.

***

With my visa sorted for the foreseeable, I felt a weight lift off my shoulders for a bit. MJ and I could relax, resume our lives and maybe even plan a holiday like regular Brits. That summer we went to Alaçatı along the Turkish coast. It was one of the very few places where South Africans could enter without having to apply for a tourist visa. Another visa, to enter another country? We had no energy for more admin.

Now Turkey was not my first choice for a summer holiday destination. It was not my second or third choice either. In fact, Turkey featured nowhere on my bucket list of travel destinations, but even I was pleasantly surprised when we arrived at Seya Beach Hotel. Think of grand sanctuary spas with high ceilings and tall indoor plants in woven baskets on sand-coloured marble tiles. The reception area was massive and smelled of tropical incense. Behind a marble desk that matched the marble floor stood three members of hotel staff who smiled at us when we approached.

"Hi, um, we're checking in today," I said, finding my passport in my purse.

"Ahh no English please," said the gentleman who pointed to his colleague next to him, who then helped us get checked in.

The gentlemen walked us through the rest of the hotel, each corridor even loftier than the one before. Our room had a view of the pool, surrounded by straw umbrellas and loungers with lush white pillows. The hotel had its own private beach with deck chairs where you could basically park yourself all day, and have your food brought to you as and when. We spent most of our days switching between the pool and the beach, and the beach bar and the pool restaurant, filling up on Vitamin D, directly from the source. It was everything I needed to forget about the co-morbidities I read about at work everyday.

Seya Beach Hotel also became the place we returned to year after year, when we needed to recharge close to home.

The pandemic

~ 2020 ~

By 2020, I had already spent two years at the startup. MJ and I were able to apply for Indefinite Leave to Remain and we had our independence day. Even though I was now free to leave the startup and get back to my dream of the Cannes Lion, I didn't resign. I also didn't look at the jobs boards to see what was out there. I wanted to take a break from the next hustle, the next interview, and to the next job, for a bit. I didn't have the pressure of needing to work to secure a visa. And I needed a minute just to decompress. I was tired and needed a recharge. My mum had just returned to Cape Town from her annual trip to London and we talked about all the holidays we wanted to take, all the beaches we wanted to go to when she came next time. We thought about Greece, Portugal and Spain and started making some lightweight plans.

I remember sitting at my desk one day and one of my coworkers explained how she might cancel her trip to Japan in June because of a new virus that everyone was talking about on the news.

"What virus?" I asked.

"Coronavirus," she said "I'm sure it will be over by June, but I think just in case, I might need to cancel my trip."

"But it's only February now," I said, "I'm sure by June it would've fizzled out already?"

"Yeah, I think so too," she said, and we continued working as usual.

A month later we saw more cases recorded and more countries reported that Coronavirus was rapidly spreading. So maybe this virus was a bit more serious than we thought? By March 2020, the World Health Organisation declared Coronavirus, or COVID-19 as it was officially named, a global pandemic. The entire world went into lockdown. Stores were forced to close. People were asked to stay at home and only leave for very limited reasons, such as seeking healthcare and buying essential food and home supplies if you could not have it delivered at home.

All the big tech companies took the mandatory work from home approach to keep their employees safe. At the startup, we were still coming into the office five days a week. I thought about emailing HR to work from home. MJ had asthma and from what we knew about the virus so far, it attacked your respiratory system. That classed MJ in the vulnerable category of the population; people who were at higher risk of Coronavirus. According to the NHS (National Health Service) of England, vulnerable adults needed to have less exposure to the outside world during the pandemic. I decided to send that email and I was granted permission to work from home for a week. That week I had one eye on my laptop and my other eye on the news. This thing was unfolding fast and no one had a clue what was going on.

We were worried about our family back home in South Africa. Here we were in a first-world country with all the protection and access to free healthcare when and if we needed it. But our families weren't that lucky. The hospitals in South Africa were overcrowded even before COVID-19. We needed to ensure our families stayed at home and stayed safe, but in our culture it was harder to enforce a no-visitors rule. People didn't understand why they couldn't visit my mum any more. My mum, being a dressmaker, had to stop her work because it involved close contact with her customers. It was all very stressful and being several miles away from them made the anxiety even worse.

Shortly after I asked for special permission to work from home because of my husband having asthma, the entire company received an email asking us to work from home for the next few weeks. Just until the virus was contained, they said. All around us, businesses were closing. Restaurants were shutting down. The economy took a nosedive and it left casualties all in its wake.

I struggled to stay focused while working from home. I didn't have my structured work environment, meetings and set lunch times. I cancelled my gym membership because the gym closed and I didn't know when I'd be able to leave my neighbourhood again. The government predicted that social distancing and other COVID-19 restrictions might continue for over 18 months. I stopped watching the news every morning. It just kept getting worse and worse. It felt like some strange kind of nightmare where we were all waiting for someone to run out and yell PUNK'D!

One afternoon, while I sat in PJs in front of my laptop, my manager at the startup texted me on Slack: "Do you have time for a quick call?"

"Yeah. But it will have to be audio, because I haven't even washed my face yet today," I responded.

Two minutes later, my mobile phone rang.

"I'm afraid we have to let you go," My manager said.

I laughed.

There was no response.

"What? Are you serious?" I eventually blurted out.

"Yes, I'm sorry. The CEO and I have discussed, and this is what we've come up with, we just can't afford to fund the marketing role any more,"

I was shocked. Disappointed. Let down, all over again.

"What have I done?" I asked.

"It's nothing you've done. And we have to thank you for all the hard work you've done for us over the last two years. It's got nothing to do with your performance, it's just what we've discussed, and this is what's best for the business. I'm really sorry."

There was nothing I could've said on that call anyway that would've changed their mind. It was what was "best for the business". I was being made redundant. Again. This time it was during the start of a global pandemic.

After the initial shock subsided, the first thought I had was that at least I already had Indefinite Leave to Remain. I didn't need a visa to stay in the country. Both MJ and I had settlement status. Small glories. But we still had bills to pay. And we needed both of our incomes to avoid becoming homeless.

A few hours later, I wrote my manager an email.

```
Hi,

Can I just ask if you've explored the option of
putting me on furlough, where you keep me on the
books and the government will pay 80% of my salary?
Did you know about this? <<A link to the COVID-19
relief program for businesses>>

I completely get that the business might be
struggling right now and I empathise. I just wish
you and the CEO had respected me enough to talk to
me about this, level with me about how the business
```

```
is taking a knock, and asked me to go on reduced
pay. Instead of throwing me out to deal with this
alone. Ironically, that goes against everything I
thought that the business stood for.

Surely any of these scenarios would've been better
than the situation you have put me in.
```

After I sent that email I also posted on my LinkedIn profile. I needed to move fast. We'd just signed a lease on a new flat rental, and because MJ was still getting paid a salary, we didn't qualify for any of the government grants. The government saw it as, we had one salary in the household, so we were granted no financial support. My post on LinkedIn detailed the nature of my situation with a link to my portfolio. I was transparent that I was just made redundant, that I knew the job market was grim right now, and that I was reaching out for help. I was begging for help from anyone. I was in the dumps. But so was everyone else. All around me people were facing lay-offs due to COVID-19. Every second post on my feed was similar to my own; someone searching for help. For a lead, an introduction, a link to a job post, anything. It was a massacre out there.

Then there was the other side of the coin: companies who made big gestures to protect their employees from the pandemic, put them on paid leave until things returned back to normal. Nike, Apple and so forth. A meme made its rounds on the Internet that read *pay attention to how companies treat their employees during this time – it speaks volumes to their core ethics.* I felt it in my bones. And maybe the startup did too. Being the brand that they are, or wanted to be, who literally placed people at the core of their value proposition, they must've realised that letting people go in the middle of a pandemic, without support, was not on-brand for them.

A day later I got a call from my manager. They saw my LinkedIn post and didn't like it. They asked me to take it down. I asked why, were they going to rehire me? No they were not, but my post was giving them bad PR. I was appalled. There they were, a business making money, trying to cut costs by cutting employees and they wanted me to take down my LinkedIn post? The post where I was trying to reach potential employers to get hired during a pandemic. I wasn't even on their payroll any more, so I'm not sure why they thought they still had the right to tell me what to do.

Nevertheless, I deleted the post. Just like I deleted them from my memory bank. The same way they were able to delete me from their staff list in an instant. In the end, I was just a line item on a budget sheet for them.

It hurt being discarded. Putting all of myself into a company and not receiving the same respect in return hurt. Moreover, I had no time to strategically think about my next move. To remember the dreams I once had and the promises I made myself when I'd be free from the constraints of a visa. I needed to jump into the next available job because well, beggars, choosers. I needed to work. I wasn't even fussy about the type of job I wanted. We had hit peak pandemic. I considered packing shelves at the local Tesco. The community spirit at essential stores was incredible to witness. The staff put their lives at risk every day to ensure that we had access to essentials. I wouldn't have minded being part of that. Apart from being creative, building culture and community was very important to me.

Meanwhile, the virus was moving closer and closer to home and started to attack more people we knew. MJ's colleague tested positive, and his entire team was asked to take a PCR (polymerase chain reaction) test. Suddenly the realisation set in. No one was immune to COVID-19. We could no longer pretend that the virus was some abstract thing that only happened to other people. Luckily we were still healthy, and our families were too, but it sure was scary living in fear of getting infected. Our peaceful daily walks in the park with Sutro also took a change of pace. I wore a face mask even outdoors, worried about bringing the virus home to MJ. If people came up to us to say hello, I'd pull Sutro away and walk the other way. People we used to socialise with became strangers. I didn't know what to tell people. I didn't want people to touch her. We hugged and kissed Sutro at home all the time and if people outside of our household touched her, it meant we needed to be conscious of that. Microbe transference. If the virus was transferable from surfaces, it was also transferable from Sutro's fur. I didn't know how to explain that concept to people. And I also didn't know how to explain to my dog that she wasn't allowed to say hello to other people any more.

I heard that in Spain you weren't even allowed to go outside because of how far and fast the virus had spread. So I counted myself lucky, being able to still walk Sutro in the park. For the most part, if you didn't turn on the news it felt like nothing much had changed, and we were all just living a little quieter. Simpler.

Each one help one

The way president Cyril Ramaphosa handled the pandemic made me truly proud to be South African. A couple of hundred cases were recorded and he announced a total lockdown. No one was allowed to leave their homes except for food or medical supplies. The people allowed to leave their homes, to continue working, were medical professionals, emergency services, military and police, essential services such as food and utilities and banking services. The president ordered all non-essential stores to close. He set up emergency water services in rural areas to help with sanitation. A fund was set up to help vulnerable South Africans and business owners, including people in informal settlements whose businesses were affected. Regulations were set up to prevent independent stores from hiking up prices and to avoid panic-buying. Homeless people were taken off the streets and put into shelters. South Africa is a country with a large divide between rich and poor. The homeless and people living in informal settlements didn't have the resources to protect themselves against the virus. But this instruction gave everyone a fighting chance to survive the virus. Ramaphosa laid out rules to protect the entire population. And it inspired business leaders to do more to give back to the community.

Many businesses handed out free hand sanitisers to people who couldn't afford it. From the comforts of my home, in a country far away from South Africa, that was heart-warming to see.

Similar actions were put in place in the UK, but with less of an urgency to follow the rules. Staying at home, social distancing and washing your hands was a suggestion from the government. Even though the numbers were soaring in the UK, our restrictions felt more like Corona-light than anything else.

Lockdown days started out with rolling out of bed, making coffee, commuting from the kitchen to my desk in the living room and starting my quest for a new job. I'd take a short break at lunchtime to walk Sutro in our local park. Sometimes MJ would join us and we'd talk anxiously about what the future held. Sometimes we'd just walk in brooding silence. Everyday felt like groundhog day. I tried to keep track of the days and do a daily check-in to record how I felt. But by day seven, I'd already lost track of the days. Outside, the streets turned emptier and quieter than the day before.

"We need TP, " MJ said as we left the house to walk Sutro.

"We can stop at Aldi on the way back." I suggested.

There was no toilet paper at Aldi, so we stopped off at Co-op. No toilet paper there either. Tesco? No toilet paper.

"Should I check online at Sainsbury's?" I asked.

"Yeah, we might have to," said MJ.

When we got home I checked online but Sainsbury's were not doing home deliveries for weeks. All the slots were booked out. We got in MJ's company car and drove to three other supermarkets we knew of in search of basic supplies but found empty shelves everywhere. People were still panic-buying despite the rationing. Each household was only allowed to buy two units of certain items, like toiletries or food essentials, at the store. For protection against the virus, stores were also limiting how many people could enter the store at a time. I saw families queue together outside the stores and pretend not to know each other inside the stores, only so that they were able to buy more items per household than the capped amount. There were apocalyptic scenes out there.

Everyone else was on the road too in search of supplies. I felt like we were in an episode of *The Walking Dead* just before everything went a little out of control. And going outside without wearing a face mask was like going out unarmed. Toilet paper had become a rare commodity. Somehow a rumour had spread that factories who made toilet paper had shut down and there'd be a shortage real soon. After searching far and wide, I turned to online shopping, but also to no avail. I then resorted to paying a very steep amount for some basic toilet paper that would only arrive the following week. The situation was becoming dire. And we were running out of funds fast.

The fear of possibly contracting the virus and trying not to breathe in the vicinity of another human being made my anxiety and OCD worse. Add to that, the stress of being unemployed and that gives you a rough idea of the head space I was in. Yet still, the word grateful always came to mind. I thought about all the people who were possibly in a worse situation than I was. I thought about people who had no roof over their heads, no food, no second income from a partner, no internet access or laptops to apply for jobs and no one to share their struggles with. Even without the prospect of a job and possibly becoming homeless next month, I certainly counted more blessings than woes. Like me, there were so many people out there struggling, people out there who'd lost their jobs due to the Coronavirus pandemic. There were so many people whose jobs could only be done in person and with the world shutting down, all those people instantly lost their income.

A few weeks ago, before I deleted my post on LinkedIn, someone shared it and included the hashtag #EachOneHelpOne. I didn't know the person who shared it. They weren't even a connection of mine on LinkedIn, but they shared my post. I also noticed something strangely wonderful starting to emerge on LinkedIn. All the unemployed people who were in the same boat as I was in, started tagging each other on job ads, posts and articles on the feed. Articles like *How to ace your next interview* and *100 resources to help you pivot and find remote jobs online* were being shared among us. We were unconsciously creating a community and sharing resources to help each other in these seriously dark times. That's when the idea came to me. What if we curated all these resources and saved them in one place for people affected by loss of income due to Coronavirus?

Without a second thought I created the Facebook group called COVID-19 Loss of Employment Support: Advice and support for people who've lost their jobs due to the Coronavirus pandemic. Everyday I posted tips and advice that I found; mostly articles about the new furlough scheme from the government and how to get your redundancy overturned. In the meantime, someone created a live spreadsheet of jobs posted globally and it was being updated in real time. I linked that spreadsheet from my group as well. Within days, the group became the first place where people went when they got that same call I got: *I'm sorry, but we have to let you go.*

If there's one thing I've learned from growing up in [12]Mzansi it is that we show up for people. We share our hardships. We pay it forward. #EachOneHelpOne. When I had no news or articles to post, I'd share words of encouragement. I wrote

```
Companies are still recruiting, no matter what
you've been told! Don't lose hope!
```

I wanted to help everyone out there get back up so we could get through this ordeal together, stronger than before. Because something good's got to come out of all of this. And when this was over, because I believed it would be over, I wanted to look back and say that I was part of the solution. There was something very fulfilling to me about being at rock bottom and using my words to lift others up. In a weird way, I found comfort, light and positivity in our collective sadness.

We lived off benefits from the state. As a permanent resident

---

[12] A colloquial term meaning "South Africa," derived from the isiXhosa and isiZulu word *umzantsi*, meaning "south".

in the UK, and with no income, I was able to apply for financial support. It was a measly amount that barely covered our rent and utilities, but it saw us through a couple of hard months. We still had MJ's salary too, but for how long, we didn't know. He was placed on furlough, as his job at British American Tobacco required him to be out in the field, visiting retail stores that were now closed. We were living month to month waiting to hear if he'd be paid furlough the next month.

With summer ending, the days were getting colder. Temperatures were already dropping in London. And because we were home all day, instead of a temperature-controlled office like the previous winter, we had to turn on our central heating in order to not freeze. But we weren't used to turning the central heating on all day. Could we even afford to? France declared an energy bill freeze for everyone in the country, so people wouldn't have to worry about their gas and electricity bills during the pandemic. In the UK, we still had to pay our bills.

The lockdowns were extended, the number of Coronavirus cases kept rising, the only hope for some kind of normal was the rollout of the vaccines.

The long pause

The world had shut its doors, and London felt like it was holding its breath. Every evening brought another law, another restriction, as we waited with bated breath for the prime minister's announcement. I stopped reading the news first thing in the morning; the dread was too heavy to carry before coffee. It was all the same; death counts, rising numbers, fear spreading faster than the virus itself. It felt like waking into a dream you cannot leave.

One day I moved from the spare room desk to the sofa, breaking my own rule. The flat was too cold. In South Africa, the sun could always be relied on to warm a room. Here, the radiators hum all day, and I wondered if we could afford this new ritual. The privilege of warmth was not a given.

Our bread was almost gone. The soap too. The last time I went to the supermarket the shelves were stripped bare, even of the vegan milk. Perhaps next time will be the same. But still, I was grateful to be able to walk through the doors and choose. My mother did not always have that luxury, and I know many still don't. I've stayed inside for more than a week. They say central London is deserted, but I haven't seen it with my own eyes. Out here in the suburbs, people kept moving, always at a distance, always cautious. Londoners were resilient like that. We have to be. And perhaps that's why I felt a strange kinship with this city: survival stitched into its seams.

But survival looks different depending on where you begin. For some, lockdown is an inconvenience. For others, it is hunger. I couldn't stop thinking about the people in South Africa where jobs vanished and there were no savings to fall back on. Here in London, tech giants donated billions, scientists chased cures in shiny labs. Back in Cape Town, survival was still hand to mouth. I lived between both realities, privileged and guilty in equal measure. And yet, a rhythm was forming. Not the old rhythm, but something slower. Less panic, less frenzy. A strange stability. When I did manage to leave the flat for groceries, MJ told me, *be safe*. Stepping into a store felt like stepping onto a battlefield. Even breathing felt dangerous. People seemed dangerous. It was like living in an episode of *The Walking Dead*: to leave the house without a mask was to walk into the world unarmed.

At least we could still walk Sutro. Short lead, quick steps, watchful eyes. People were still trying to pet her and I found myself yelling, "keep your distance" —my voice sounding foreign, sharp, like I'm protecting more than just the dog. I knew this too will pass. The only way out was through. One day the city will glow again, its lights sharp against the night sky, and we'll stand in the streets, breathing freely. My only wish was that when we returned to life, it would not be to the same life we left behind. I hoped it won't be at the expense of the planet we've watched begin to heal in our absence.

The pandemic changed a lot of people's perspectives on life. But not mine. Being an introvert with mild OCD became trendy. Finally, I could wash my hands in public bathrooms without being stared at because I'd take longer than the average person to wash my hands. I could open doors with my elbow/foot without the fear of someone catching me in the act, because it was apparently 'normal' to do that during a pandemic. I could hold onto the pole on the tube with some item of clothing to avoid direct contact with my skin and somehow it didn't seem so strange any more. Neither did opting out of a handshake immediately. I'd been preparing for this my whole life.

* * *

In December 2020, the world was slowly starting to open up. I heard some people were travelling abroad again. I heard it was strange, masks everywhere, COVID-19 vaccine passes upon entry, a lot of pandemic policing. It was a different world out there than the one we used to know.

Two weeks before our flight to Cape Town, a scientist in South Africa identified a new Coronavirus variant. The virus had already mutated dozens of times, as viruses do, and that's what made this one more contagious. They'd also tested the new variant and discovered that it was more immune to the vaccines. And it was spreading rapidly across South Africa. The World Health Organisation called it Omicron. I was worried for my family in South Africa. Hospitals were overcrowded, treatment was a luxury, and the virus had already taken far too many familiar names from us. Who would be next? We were longing to be with our families, but at the same time they urged us not to come, begged us to stay in London and be safe.

The next day, travel bans were introduced. The United Kingdom, Europe and the entire global north banned all travel to and from South Africa. The UK had a traffic light system, which meant people were still able to travel to green and amber countries. But if the country was on the red list, travel to that country was prohibited. They placed South Africa on the red list. So even if we wanted to, we couldn't leave the country to see our families. We were not allowed.

"Let's just wait two weeks and postpone our flights, this will be over soon," I wanted to believe. MJ didn't believe me.

I was angry at the media for portraying South Africa as the country where Omicron came from. It was lazy journalism and factually incorrect. Scientists in South Africa identified a new strain of the virus, shared that information with the world, and the media was crucifying them for it. The media neglected to report that Omicron was already present in the UK, New Zealand and Europe. And so the world hysterically blamed South Africa and failed to give them the credit they deserved for identifying the new strain.

South Africa has one of the best epidemiology infrastructures in the world. For decades, we've had to deal with AIDS and Tuberculosis. Some of the world's leading experts in infectious diseases work in South Africa so they're able to identify new variants quickly. South African scientists were the first to identify Omicron, sequenced it, began to understand it and have shared that information with the world. In return, an indefinite travel ban leading to billions lost in the tourism economy. Thousands of flights were cancelled, including ours. The travel ban hit us hard. Every South African living abroad wondered the same thing that year: *will I ever get to see my family again?*

With no permanent job on the horizon because of the pandemic, I tried to find ways to turn more of our things into cash. It was an arduous process trying to get our refund from the cancelled flights to Cape Town. I procrastinated in doing this too because I secretly hoped that the cancelled flights would become un-cancelled and we could still go to Cape Town. A flight from London to Cape Town averaged £800 per person. Minus taxes, handling fees, COVID-19 admin fees, we only got some of it back. And that's when I decided to never ever book a flight via a cheap travel website ever again.

Like many people whose income was affected during the pandemic, we were forced to count our pennies. We made little changes to downgrade our lifestyle. Not like we were living extravagantly anyway, but the little things made a difference. Like swapping barista coffee for instant, cooking more with cheaper ingredients instead of ordering take-out every second day. MJ's furlough would come to an end soon, he was job searching too. I had a writing gig contract for a couple of months but nothing permanent and no prospects either. Being a contractor wasn't easy. Everything was temporary. No matter how long my contract would be renewed for, the end date always hovered overhead. I was caught in a constant, never-ending struggle to do better than my best, to exceed my role expectations so that my employer would notice and offer me a permanent position. This meant that when I had interviews scheduled, I'd hit the reserve energy, which often was not my best self. My professional confidence was at an all-time low. The pickings for jobs were slim to none. No one was hiring during an economic and global health crisis. Between the rejections, the ghosting from the few applications I managed to get in, and the video interviews that all went badly, I had no confidence in my abilities any more. But I knew that I needed to at least try to believe in myself again because if I didn't, nobody else would.

One step at a time, I thought. I needed to get back on track. And if I couldn't do it for myself, I needed to remember to do it for the people who depended on me.

Overthinking in technicolour

I know many people felt depressed during the pandemic, because of loss of jobs, loss of freedom, loss of health and loved ones. I wasn't depressed. My type A personality turned towards an anxious brain instead of a depressed one. I needed to fix it, and the lack of control heightened my anxiety. I'd wake up and even after one cup of coffee, I'd get heart palpitations. Every email made me nervous. Every call made me jump. The unpredictability of life had shaken me.

In psychology, OCD (Obsessive-Compulsive Disorder) is a mental health condition where the brain gets stuck in a loop of intrusive thoughts (obsessions) and repetitive behaviours (compulsions). The obsessions are unwanted thoughts, fears or images that cause distress. Compulsions are the actions or rituals people do to reduce the anxiety around the thoughts.

I've been living with an undiagnosed case of anxiety and OCD for years and being at home with my own thoughts for long periods of time during the pandemic led to my anxiety becoming more exaggerated. I picked up this "habit" of washing my hands twice after using the loo. Think about the taps in the bathroom for a second. You do your business, you open the tap (your hands are dirty at this point) you wash your hands and close the (dirty) tap. Are your hands still clean? No, right? Logically, the answer is no (?)

So my routine of double washing my hands has become so ingrained in me that it felt normal. At home, when I'm done in the bathroom, I washed my hands a second time at the kitchen sink. The second time made them clean. In public places, malls, the office, restaurants it was a bit more challenging.

An average morning getting ready for work became exhausting for me. I'd shower, turn off the lights and closed the bathroom door, and I'd need to wash my hands again. Touching surfaces meant I need to wash my hands again. One morning, I grabbed my make-up bag and attempted to apply foundation. I accidentality dropped my blending sponge on the floor. We've walked through this spot of the house with shoes on, so I couldn't account for the cleanliness of the floor. I picked up my sponge, went back to the kitchen to wash it, then washed my hands again. Before I returned to what I was doing, I heard dripping in the bathroom and saw that I didn't close the tap properly. You know what happened next..

Almost every time I left the house, I felt annoyed that I was late. I promised myself that I'd be earlier the next day. It never happened. One morning, I put on my AirPods while walking to the tube and dropped the case on the pavement. I froze. People looked at me. I'd seen dog poo there before - not today, not yesterday, not even last week. And it had rained for days. Logically, I knew the pavement wasn't contaminated. But that's the thing about OCD: logic doesn't silence the whispers.

My brain is like a hyperactive smoke alarm - it goes off more often than it should. It keeps me safe, but it's exhausting when it won't quiet down.

I contemplated leaving my AirPods case on the ground, but it's not cheap so reluctantly I picked it up. I put it in the tote bag. I walked the rest of the way not letting the tote bag touch my body. I know when I got to the office I'll use the anti bac wipes to wipe every single item in my tote bag that may have just been in close proximity to the AirPods case. I'm not sure if I can put my pods back in the case. The jury is still out. I need to Google the price of a replacement case, that'll be the deciding factor.

I know normal people don't agonise over germs the way I do. I know I'm not normal. But what is normal anyway?

OCD isn't really about dirt or germs though, it's about doubt. The obsession is the brain whispering, "What if?" What if the pavement is contaminated, what if touching it means I'll carry that risk with me all day? The compulsion is my attempt to quiet the whisper - wiping, separating, cleaning, avoiding. It's a nightmare living in my head.

I didn't want to take medication because I already had an unhealthy habit of zombifying myself when in a state of trauma, I didn't need any more numbing aids. I was all good. I needed a holistic way to deal with this constant zinging of wild thoughts that wouldn't leave me alone. With everything going a mile a minute in my head, I needed to slow down. MJ wondered why I started listening to soft, acoustic music everyday instead of the thrashing guitars and drums of my punk rock playlist.

"It soothes me," I said.

"Sellout," MJ laughed.

The gentle sounds of The Lovely Little Playlist, The Stress Buster and, lately, the piano sounds of Music for Writing from Spotify helped to create a sense of calm inside my head. The more I learned, the more changes I made to my lifestyle. And this looked like, protein breakfast in the morning to stabilise hormones and reduce the heart-palpitation effects of caffeine on an empty stomach. It was swapping my stressful cardio routine for a slower hot yoga to help me to focus only on the moment. A friend on Instagram introduced me to the Turtle app for counting macronutrients, not calories. Knowing exactly how much macronutrients, protein, carbs and fat, is needed to fuel my body changed the game for my physical and mental health. Religiously tracking my macros meant I was eating to fuel my body instead of satisfying my sugar cravings. The result was immediate; no more fatigue and less anxiety attacks.

Being present eased my worry about the unknown. Walking with Sutro in the park, I relearned how to breathe. Every small measure I took to slow down taught me something new. In brown culture, mental health isn't prioritised — anxiety is left untreated, and many of us suffer quietly. I see it in my mum when deadlines or complex wedding dress designs overwhelm her. She names the symptoms, but it's clearly anxiety. And since the pandemic, it feels like we've all carried a little of that anxiety with us.

Apartheid caused major disparities in access to healthcare. As a result, many people of colour didn't have the support or information to help them identify mental health conditions. Our people aren't educated about the complexities of mental health, so we never seek support. And we repeat this cycle year after year with every new person of colour born into the family.

My family never spoke about mental health. We were taught to pray or "be strong" because I come from a long line of strong women. This created an environment where the absence of words like anxiety and OCD was the standard. Silence was the cultural baseline. I learned about mental health first in advertising; where my colleagues spoke casually about therapy, mental health days and burnout. This was in direct contrast to my own instinct to swallow pain, to keep working harder.

It took me over 30 years to recognise that my obsessive hand washing, fear of germs, door-checking and need for reassurance in the details were symptoms of OCD. And now, knowing more about my condition, I am able to manage it and advocate for myself. In Cape Town, these quirks were quirks. People around me laughed it off and joked about it to my face. In London, I am encouraged to language the emotions I feel when intrusive thoughts happen, I am encouraged to learn more about it, accept it and learn how to manage the anxiety that comes with it. I am never shamed for it.

I realised resilience isn't the absence of fragility, and silence protects no one. Maybe the first step toward healing was the moment I whispered the truth to a friend, googled therapy, or simply admitted to myself: *I am not okay.*

Take only what you need

With 19 days left of 2020, I felt reflective. I looked back on the year and all the changes that life threw at us. COVID-19 was the biggest plot twist of the century. Everyday we waited for an update of when the borders would reopen, when we would be able to see our families again. As soon as we would be able to travel again, I wouldn't take for granted the time I'd get to spend with my family. I wanted to appreciate every moment. I hoped it was not too late.

2020 came with many lessons for a lot of people. Personally, the year taught me how to get by with a little less than I used to. With so much access to the modern world, it's easy to buy into the comforts of consumerism. Buy 20 dresses just to try them all on at home and send back 19. But the returns never make it back on the shelves. Instead they end up in a landfill, polluting the planet. So where I would've done that in the past, I now take only what I need. Because the Earth's resources are not in abundance, and we were already living on borrowed time.

When the lockdown happened I hoarded a lot of food. This made me conscious of how much trash I created, and how much I contributed towards global warming. But if I took only what I needed, I was forced to use up what's already in my home before buying more food that might go to waste.

One of my neighbours told me about an app called Olio. It's where people could share items and produce they'd want to get rid of, like furniture, food, clothes, literally anything. So I put a lot of things up for grabs on the app, and I met a lot of people that way too. It gave our unwanted items, that would've usually ended up in a landfill, a chance at a second life. Too many people have been affected by the pandemic, with job losses, reduced hours and loss of homes. Olio was a good way to help the community while also reducing our carbon footprint.

I was still lacking a permanent job. But I loved the work I was doing on myself, as a person, to heal, to reduce my contribution to consumerism, to be present in a city where you're constantly overstimulated and to be more conscious of my impact on the planet.

All we have is now

~ 2021 ~

Another year living in the pandemic. At the start of the year, MJ got that fateful call too. His company couldn't afford to keep paying their team, so his entire team was let go. This also meant he had to give up his company car and we had to start paying for travel again to commute anywhere. I was still mostly unemployed, going from contract to contract. Permanent jobs were hard to come by when the global economy was so unstable. And we had no family in the country to fall back on. We just couldn't catch a break, could we?

I checked in with the Facebook support group I created and the situation hadn't changed much from the previous year. Jobs were still scarce. Many people had to pivot from their actual profession and do something else just to earn an income. I posted again:

```
For those of you who are thinking, you have no
income because your job is compromised, you won't
get paid for taking time off work or your job is not
one that can be done remotely... listen up, find
something else to do. This is your calling, your
second chance. Learn a new trade or hobby. What if
this is the fresh start you wish you had? What if
this is the beginning of something better for you,
something that feels more authentic to who you
really are. You can do anything you want. Make your
own plan B.
```

As the founder of the group, people were enthused when I wrote and would send lots of heart reactions and that energised me. The post, as always, was a reflection of what I was feeling that week. I too was thinking about living a more purposeful life. I thought about my big dream to make it in ad land, to win a Cannes Lion, to see my work on television. None of that mattered any more. I didn't care about making ads any more. There were more important things in life than making ads. I didn't know where that left me, to be honest. What would I do if I couldn't make ads? My mum's voice lingered in my head; the thing she told me when she convinced me to study copywriting instead of design.

"With a Journalism diploma, you can do any type of writing you want. You have so many options."

***

It snowed in London that February. The world as we knew it

didn't exist any more. With the lockdown, there were less cars on the road, less planes in the sky and less fossil fuels polluting the air around us. Mother Earth was getting a reset.

We were reconstructing our lives around a new kind of normal. And while doing this, the planet could finally heal. The world shifted back into equilibrium. Scientists reported that the damage to the ozone layer was slowly being reversed. But only a little bit. We still needed to do our part to delay global warming as much as we could. Wildlife were reclaiming their spaces all over the world. Even deep down inside, my soul felt a little cleaner. Like I was more connected to nature. My yearning for the superficial glory of ad land started to feel irrelevant.

Liz and I still tried to meet up when we could. In the quiet streets of central London we walked, a slower pace than we would in a different lifetime. In a pre-pandemic London. The shops on the high street were open, but empty. Big, red »Closing Down Sale« banners across the glass windows.

"Oh man, another one who didn't survive the pandemic," I said.

"Yeah, it's sad isn't it?" said Liz.

When we reached Dishoom, there was a cluster of people waiting outside. At least Dishoom survived the pandemic. We entered the restaurant and followed the waiter to a corner table. Liz always knew the best places to eat. I would never have guessed that an Indian restaurant also served a great breakfast;

but their chilli cheese toast and vegan sausage naan roll proved me wrong.

"So what's the job?" Liz asked.

I was exploring applying for a role as a content designer. It was a full time position, and I wanted Liz's opinion.

For someone with a marketing and social media background, content design wasn't a term I'd heard very often. Sure, I studied copywriting, started out as a writer but over the years, I'd honed my craft in content strategy: formulating a plan for the creation, delivery and governance of long-form or social content. What I'd done for brands over the years was plan and create branded content for their owned digital and social channels. A content strategy is the cornerstone of brand marketing; it ensures that every piece of content in the experience serves and sustains a legitimate purpose, and perpetuates the promise that brands want consumers to believe in. Product content strategy, or content design, is a different kind of strategy that lends some of the same principles but is more user-experience focused. Content design is thinking about the experience, or the user flow, before the content is written. In short, it focuses on how best to communicate the information needed for a user to navigate through an app, website or product flow. Many content designers came from marketing backgrounds. As content strategists, we're trained to help move people through a funnel - to get them where we want them to go, whatever the goal of the piece of content you put out there may be. So it's not uncommon for marketing content strategists to make the switch to content design.

Some don't ever switch; they just do both. In fact, well-known Content Design London states that content design is for every style of communication; and doesn't limit the discipline to a product's user interface. It could be for a product, service, website, social media, marketing and advertising. Still, content design for products in the tech industry sounded like the shift in focus I needed.

"It's like, user experience content strategy… user experience design. I'll work with a designer and together we'd create the user flows for how people use a website or an app. So all the words that you see on a website, how the information is organised, the labels on a button, what happens when you click the button and all that experience design stuff… that's done by a content designer," I relayed my understanding of content design to Liz.

"Oh, it sounds really interesting," she said encouragingly.

"Yeah it's different to what I'm used to. I don't think I'm qualified for the role at all," I laughed.

"Ahh, that's not true. You're a copywriter, so you know how to write. You know what works and what doesn't. You know what a good user experience looks like," Liz explained.

"But I write marketing content, hah."

"I think you're qualified for it, babe."

"Thanks, Liz,"

"All done?" A waiter interrupted.

"Yeh, you can take this, thanks," Liz replied.

"Should we get dessert?" I asked.

"Oof, go on then,"
 We shared a plate of sweet uttapam pancakes, topped with cream, berries and coconut flakes. It tasted as dreamy as it sounds.

As we left the restaurant and walked towards the tube station, Liz again encouraged me to go for the job. Even after years had passed, and a pandemic later, she still had that magnetic power to lift my mood. I was grateful for her friendship, and as we parted ways I wondered if she knew.

Waiting for the tube on the platform felt somewhat nostalgic. Just like the streets above, the Underground too seemed eerily quiet that day. It was sad to see London this way. One of the busiest and touristy places in the world, deserted.

I thought back to how I used to spend two hours a day commuting to work, crammed in the middle of a metal tube underground, just to clock into an office before 8:30am. None of that was a reflection of your productivity. Now we had all this free time. And knowing that time was fleeting, I wondered what I could do with my extra time. I wanted to do something meaningful. All around me, people were waking up to this new reality. To how little control we really had. All we really had was now, to do the things we loved, to tell people we loved them, to appreciate the world we were lucky to live in. To be better than we were before.

The shift forced us to realise that we as humans did not own this planet. We were merely guests and we needed to respect the Earth and all beings we shared it with. Was this a wake up call? For sure. Here, we had an opportunity to truly do something extraordinary for Mother Earth, its beings and for humanity. But as we headed out of this pandemic, would we?

The self-care accounts I followed on Instagram told me that many people struggled with lockdown fatigue. After several months of working contract jobs on my own, alone in our living room, I started to feel it too. I missed the days where I was part of a team, where working from home was a special treat that I looked forward to once a week. I missed the commute to work, knowing the London Underground like the back of my hand. I missed stopping at my favourite coffee shop for overpriced coffee. I missed wandering through the city not having a particular place to go. I missed shopping on the high street. I missed conversations. I guess I missed consumerism. But I know that the way we used to exploit the planet and its resources before was selfish, and an unsustainable way to live. I just missed some form of normal life, whatever that meant. Did that make me a bad person?

As the tube approached I continued to get lost in my own thoughts, getting on the third carriage from the back, taking an empty seat towards the end of the carriage like autopilot. Then came the familiar voice of the lady who does the announcements,

"This is a Northern Line service via Charing Cross terminating at Morden."

I thought back to two summers earlier, to my holiday in Ibiza with my mum. I remember my mum being completely in awe of the island and me being a typical nonchalant faux Londoner. I didn't appreciate the moments we shared together, in a country that we never ever dreamed of visiting together. Not in a million years. I took all those precious moments for granted. Sipping mocktails by the pool together, eating fresh fish and chips by the ocean, getting lost in the old town and swimming in the Mediterranean. I choked down tears wondering if I'd ever get the opportunity to do that again with my mum.

The morning commute, a cup of coffee, the smallest mundane things

By the summer of 2021, we had spent so long in lockdown that I didn't know how to act with some of the restrictions lifted. For starters, face masks and social distancing were no longer mandatory. I still felt cautious, and didn't react to the change immediately. I passed the time lazing in my garden with Sutro and a good murdery book. I read 72 books that year. Getting lost in a different character's life was somewhat distracting from the daily struggles of "Dear Hiring Manager, please hire me." It was very therapeutic. I didn't end up getting the job as Content Designer, but after that interview I knew that was the only job I wanted more than anything else in the world. So for the next six months, I set out on a mission to upskill myself in the art of content design. I did a free online course, I read books, I spoke to people who were already doing the job, I read so many documents about processes and design thinking, so that when I reapplied for the job, I would be sure to get it.

Spending so much time in the sun made me miss summer in Cape Town. Summers in London was the only time when I missed Cape Town. I really disliked London in the summer because it was too hot, the air was too thick. The city wasn't built for warm weather. You don't fully realise how much growing up near the ocean influences your life, until you leave home for a place without the ocean. Only then does it register that summer to you means something entirely different. It's walking barefoot on sandy beaches and building elaborate sand castles with your kid cousins. It's climbing boulders at the beach to find the penguin colony swimming in a secluded pool. It's the smell of seaweed. It's *"a lolly to make you jolly"* on Clifton 4th beach. It's the shark alarm at Surfers Corner. It's that last vanilla swirly cone with a flake on the Muizenberg shoreline, with hoodies pulled over your face to block out the wind, the offshore wind that makes this one of the best surfing spots in the city. Summer is the way your hair curls naturally as it dries from a day in the sun. It's damp cotton shirts clinging to your swimsuit. It's sticky fingers clutching freshly-cut watermelon, and late evenings around the fire, listening to the waves crash as the sun sets. I hoped that we would get to experience a summer in Cape Town again.

Then the leaves changed to signify Autumn. MJ, Sutro and I took the tube to Victoria for a Sunday city stroll and lunch. It was a cool summer afternoon, where you could still walk around without a t-shirt but the air didn't suffocate you. The plan was to have lunch at one of the dog-friendly restaurants that had expanded onto the courtyards between the high rises near Victoria station. Al fresco dining was what they called it, and more and more restaurants were doing it. A lovely by-product of the pandemic. The virus still existed, but somehow dining outdoors with fresh air gave people enough comfort to start returning to restaurants. I liked that restaurants were able to open again. It was a good sign.

Everyone had the same idea. Everyone wanted a piece of normal too, and the courtyards were packed with people. It felt like old London, from before the world changed. We sat for hours in the breezy weather, having our meal and enjoying the world passing by around us. Being outside was nice and void of all COVID-19 stress. It was also one of the very few days that I bothered to get dressed and leave the house. My usual Sunday consisted of waking at 8:30am, having a coffee while video calling my mum in South Africa, writing something for the blog, walking Sutro before lunch, cooking lunch and then retiring on the sofa with Netflix. It was what we did every Sunday, apart from the Sundays when I'd meet Liz for brunch.

One such Sunday, we met for pancakes near London Bridge. After a visit to Yayoi Kusama's Infinity Rooms at the Tate, we strolled to The Table, a cosy local brunch spot, and found a table near the window.

"Happy belated birthday babes," Liz said as she handed me a teal gift bag with pink flamingos printed on the side.

"Oh my God, Liz! You really shouldn't have. Thank you so much!" I accepted the gift bag awkwardly. I love gifts, but I am a horrible gift receiver, in the fact that I never know how to behave when receiving gifts.

Liz always gets me good gifts. She knows me so well. Inside the gift bag are a few items from & Other Stories, lush products that I'd never buy myself because I'm too cheap, and The Comfort

Book by Matt Haig.

"I love it," I squealed.

"Have you heard of that book?" She asked.

"It's been on my list for ages. " I felt a little teary as I thanked Liz again.

I ran my fingers across the colourful, matte hardback cover, reading the summary. A book filled with 200+ quotes to comfort you and suggestions for making the bad days better. I flipped through some of the pages, scanning the words.

"It's okay to be the teacup with a chip in it. That's the one with a story."

I already love it, I thought. It's the most beautiful book I'd ever owned.

"So what are your options, if your contract doesn't get extended?" Liz asked, snapping me back into the present.

"I'm interviewing at a few companies, so I'm just waiting to hear back. One of them is TikTok. Lol, I don't think I'm the right age for TikTok though. Baha."

I tell her more about the job and we laugh about the ridiculousness of interview questions. They don't give you a good signal of whether someone's really good at the job or not. I realise that the two hours every other month that Liz and I spend together make up some of the happiest times of my life. Throughout my struggles with interviews, jobs and redundancies in London, Liz has been the one constant through it all. The one other constant, apart from MJ of course. I'm lucky to still have her in my life. We ask for the bill, get our coats and make our way out of the restaurant.

"So good seeing you, babe. Good luck with the interviews, and keep me posted!" Liz said.

"I will. Always good seeing you! Thanks again for the birthday gifts, you really shouldn't have," I said as we hugged goodbye.

I headed towards London Bridge Underground station, passing Borough Market. I decided to take a little detour and see what the market looked like these days. Emptier than usual, I noticed. Less face masks spotted. Still smells amazing, I thought, as I passed the truffle stand and the cheese barrel. I made a mental note to bring my mum here when she came to visit us again. We will get to do these things again, I noted.

I exited the market and walked back towards the station, tapping my oyster card on the turnstiles as I disappeared amongst the crowd. Things almost felt a little normal right then, the way they felt pre-pandemic. Walking down the escalator without a mask on felt normal, getting on the tube without a mask on felt normal, reading my book with someone breathing over my shoulder felt weird but normal. London was reopening and I couldn't help feeling a bit wistful about it. These were the little things I was hoping to experience again; the tiny details of life in this big city that I'd fallen in love with.

The minute I walked out of that plane in London, I saw my life differently. Romanticised. I guess because after 30 plus years in the same town, I was doing things for the first time again, in London. The morning commute, a cup of coffee, the smallest mundane things became a new experience for me — a world of firsts. With the lockdowns finally ending, I looked forward to experiencing new firsts again, with MJ and Sutro, in the new city we called home.

Two years without a permanent job

~ 2022 ~

Today, the Prime Minister announced an end to all COVID-19 restrictions in the United Kingdom. The virus was still around but with the rollout of vaccines, we would learn to live with it, like we do with all other infectious diseases. Many jobs would now be saved and for that I was really pleased. I also wondered whether it was too soon for us to resume normal life again. London has always been one of the busiest cities in the world, which made it a breeding ground for COVID-19. Was this it? Was it over? Could we exhale now?

The travel bans were lifted a few months ago, and we were able to visit South Africa to see our families after two years in some form of lockdown. It was a different kind of trip. I cherished all the moments. I'd remember the days on the beach, for sure, but also the in-between moments. The days I sat at that dark wood kitchen table that had seen many Friday family nights, laughing with aunty Dicka and my twin cousins, plotting how we'd avoid opening the door for visitors because we all hated making meaningless conversation.

Those late afternoons driving to Fancy Pantry with my cousin Rifaat, who has an expensive taste for gourmet sweets. Also that new dessert bar at the Waterfront, and the best burger of my life, that one night with him, MJ and Bala, at the place that we'll keep our secret.

That morning at Primi with Saara, getting to know the grown up, adult person she's become. All the days I lazed, slept and made Adeela and Zahier's house my home. And of course, the new family nights at Kent Road that now includes the cousin's partners, the youngest Williams' baby boys and my mum's new husband, Ish and his son Laeeq. We're the real Modern Family. I feel privileged to have so many people in my life who care about me and MJ.

Most of those moments were made at the same house where I spent my angsty youth, the same house where I saw my dad's dead body being carried out to the cemetery. The nights we spent there on our last visit to Cape Town fill me with so much happiness that I don't see sadness any more when I think of that house. My mum was also able to visit us in London again. And I'm excited for all the trips we still get to plan together in the near future.

* * *

2022 was the start of the endemic. I've always wondered what life would be like post-COVID-19. I never imagined that I'd ever be able to enjoy a coffee on the side walk of a restaurant in Soho again. That I'd be able to hug my friends again without a mask on. That the iconic Oxford Circus would still be a place I could enjoy people watching even after all this time. I never imagined that food markets would make a comeback, but they are thriving. I also never thought I'd see planes flying over my head every ten minutes again, or that I'd get lost in a sea of people on the platform at Bank station without wearing a mask. That we'd be able to socialise with other dog owners again in our local park. Or even that toilet paper would return to store shelves and their net value would decrease again. That year, I was really looking forward to exploring all the Christmas markets around South Bank again. But with my mum this time. I almost think that the world has returned to normal. Whether that's a good thing, I still don't know.

MJ got a new job at a company he loves and who loves him back. He made a complete 180 in his career. I guess he took my advice that I posted in the COVID-19 support group. *You can be anything you want to be.* Not everyone gets a chance to start over, but he did and I couldn't be happier or more proud. He's doing really well.

And me? Being a freelancer during the COVID-19 pandemic tested me in ways that are unimaginable. I've had to push harder than I've ever done to secure a job, and then keep the job or work hard to get my contract extended. The uncertainty that comes with short-term contracts, especially during a period of global uncertainty wears you down. If you have no savings or financial safety net, then a part of you is always going to be thinking of that next job, the next hustle, the next interview. It's like part of your brain is always out of focus, like a nagging migraine. So many times I wished that I could switch off the hustle and just focus on doing great work at my contract job; I really just wanted the luxury of losing myself in the work problem and focus on making great things. But it's survival mode, and you can't turn that off. The lesson I learned from that experience was mental resilience, and that's something I can take with me for the rest of my life. Resilience is not something we're born with. It's something we build up by dealing with stressful situations and setbacks, such as loss of income, a global pandemic or death of a family member. Building resilience won't eliminate the problems we might face, but it will give us the strength to see past them and find joy in life irrespective of our problems.

After two years of freelancing and the job market still not stabilising, I wasn't sure if I would ever get a permanent job again. All the interviews I did indicated that most agencies weren't ready to commit to hiring full time employees again. There was too much risk. Instead they were hiring on a project or client basis, so mostly 3-6 month contracts with the possibility of becoming permanent. By now I already knew that possibility was very slim. But I trusted the journey and I knew that there'd be something out there for me.

The truth about being mixed race

For my 37th birthday I treated myself to something that truly nourished my broken soul: a 23andme DNA kit, to help me understand my mixed identity, and therapy for my anxiety and OCD. My weekly therapy sessions have been the best decision I've made for myself. I go away from each session with more knowledge about the inner workings of my brain and my inner self. Neuroimaging studies suggest that people with OCD have distinct differences in their brain structure — it's what make it possible for the condition to exist. A brain with OCD present shows up wildly different on an MRI than a brain with no OCD present.

"I wish I had a normal brain," I tell her.

"No one has a normal brain." She responds.
I like her, I decide.

I talk about everything, about my experiences in London and in Cape Town. I tell her things I never imagined I'd be telling a stranger. But I'm getting better at advocating for myself and making the effort to heal. It's still new to me, treating a mental health condition. I don't remember the exact moment that I felt my anxiety become so overwhelming. Probably around the time when life was so uncertain, with visa applications and job interviews on loop. There are a lot of free therapy programs and online support forums out there. NABS is an independent charity organisation set on embedding mental wellness within the advertising industry. That was the first time I heard that I can speak to someone professionally about anxiety. I guess with the internet, social media and COVID-19, everyone developed a little anxiety.

I'm not oblivious to the role that ad agency life played in my developing anxiety. And leaving it, or being forced to leave it via my role being made redundant, was a blessing in disguise. I know the industry has changed since then. It was twelve years ago when I just started out and we're seeing more people of colour in positions that were only filled by White professionals in the past. But sadly, the agency environment has not changed. A few scrolls on the Instagram account @agency_insider and you'll know what I mean. Stories like mine exist in every country and it's not worth calling out names because it is the vast majority of agencies. Of course, there are outliers and there are agencies who value their staff. But they are exactly that, outliers. If you love the idea of working in an agency, may you find these outliers and may you be them.

The best way to describe the creative process at an agency is not my own. Several versions have emerged of this concept since Luke Sullivan first published it in his book "Hey Whipple, Squeeze This - A guide to creating great ads". The version below is by far my favourite, written by an unknown author on LinkedIn.

```
The creative process is like "washing a pig." What
on earth does that mean? Well, it's an absurd
process, with no beginning, no end, and no rules.

Let's say your account person tells you they need a
pig washed by 3pm tomorrow - this is the
"advertisement" your client needs. You quickly jump
online and search in vain for a guide on pig washing
- this is your hunt for ideas and inspiration. But
you've never washed a pig before, so despite the
instructions, your first attempts fail and the pig
gets away every time - just like coming up with
ideas that never seem good enough.

It's nearing 2pm. and your partner has just figured
out how to keep the pig in place by feeding it
vanilla wafers. Finally, you've got it pretty clean
- this is when your idea thankfully seems to be
working. But then at 3pm, in comes your client. He
says that he actually needs a warthog washed - and
that's when you discover that all your work was
useless and you have to start over from the
beginning.
```

This scenario can only exist if people are not valued and if managers allow their staff to be exposed to this type of treatment. In my career, I became the head of the content department, I was good enough to get transferred to London - the creative hub of the world - then became the agency's only Creative Director. I was performing at my peak every single day, creating excellent work, but inside I was so depressed, burnt-out and stressed. That culture is celebrated in an agency, and I'm sorry that it took me 12 years to realise that this is not normal.

I was determined to find companies with better managers, a better culture and better support. Companies where my worth would be celebrated. I can now tell you with all honesty and certainty that these companies do exist.

When I got my 23andMe ancestry results back, I thought I'd be more surprised. I spent hours analysing the data. All those years growing up I had this feeling in my gut that I was not brown, a complete whole colour. I've always related more to being mixed race. That feeling makes sense now more than ever. Looking at my results, I am the epitome of what mixed race stands for. 14.6% Filipino and Austronesian. 12.8% French and German. Those are the most dominant parts of my DNA. But really, I'm from everywhere. My full ancestral composition is made up of 34 different regions around the world, with less than 1% being South African. Instead I am 32.9% Central and South Asian split into Bengali, Sri Lankan, Malayali and more, 25.6% East Asian split into Filipino, Indonesian, Thai, Myanmar, Chinese, Taiwanese and Austronesian, 22.9% European split into French, German, Irish and British (not enough to claim citizenship though, hah), 2.7% Western Asian and North African split into Iranian, Caucasian and Mesopotamian, Arab, Egyptian, Levantine, and only 11% being Sub Saharan African which is split into so many fractions: 9% Congolese, 1.8% Southern East African, 0.1% Nigerian, 0.5% Broadly West African and 0.2% Sudanese. My DNA paints the perfect picture of the rich cultural history of South Africa. And I think many of South African people of colour share a similar DNA painting.

The Dutch used South Africa as their slave trade hub, but they really colonised many parts of the world. So they transported people from region to region, mostly from Pacific Islands to Africa, where the Austronesian in my DNA comes from. Every Coloured person in South Africa has a different story and a different heritage. But the government grouped us all together as one race: non-whites. At least now I can say that I'm part of a long line of mixed race people, with ancestors from the Pacific Islands. I can't relate to the French and German part of my DNA, as I know this probably comes from the western men who slept with my slave ancestors. They were White; I'm not White. I've never benefited from the privileges that come with being White. I've always been Coloured, mixed race, the descendant of slaves.

I do wonder what my ancestors' lives were like when they were brought over as prisoners on those boats that sailed across the ocean from the islands. When they left their homes, what did they leave behind, who did they leave behind? Did they ever manage to go back? What happened to their children, their families? What would their lives be like if they weren't captured as part of the slave trade? Their stories should and need to be told.

For girls like me

It's the summer of 2022, the summer in London. It's the first year that I am able to appreciate summer in the city, and I start to realise why everyone loves summers in London. With a new sense of appreciation for the everyday, I try to do all the summery things I can because I know that summer too will soon pass. These late sunsets at 10pm, the early morning park walks with Sutro, the warm sunshine on my back in the afternoon, restaurant diners spilling out onto the pavements, these will all soon pass when the leaves on the trees turn brown and yellow again this year.

My favourite place in the summer is still our garden room with Sutro laying at my feet. I reflect on my epic journey.

"Hey Portal, play the lovely playlist," I say.

"Okay, here's *The Lovely Little Playlist* from Spotify," my Meta Portal responds and creates the ambience I love by playing my and Sutro's favourite laid-back playlist.

Sutro turns to me and gives me a side-eye look with her questioning expression. I like to believe that when she does this, she means to say "Settle down on the sofa, so we can both relax".

I pull the blanket over my knees, open my laptop and I scratch her belly.

"My little baby poopy," I say to her.

She responds with her usual piglet grunts. This dog has been by my side more times than most humans have. She came into our lives when I was battered and broken, struggling with my dad's death and she was the love that I needed to fill the hollow spaces. She taught me how to run again, be free again, and let go. She taught me how to enjoy the outdoors, to listen for the silence between the trees. She stuck her head out the car window with me when we took joyrides through the coastlines. She was there when I got the news about my move to London and when I immediately turned it down because I didn't think we could move continents without her, but we figured it out in the end. She's seen so many flats with us in London as we figured out which one we'd make our home. She sat quietly next to me when I cried over visa applications that didn't pan out, and getting rejected from so many job interviews after I got laid off during the pandemic. She's pulled me out of an anxiety attack when no one knew I was having one; being high-functioning sucks. She's seen me at my best and also at my worst.

My eyes blur with emotion as I think about how many years this dog has been walking excitedly by my side. She's put on a little bit of weight since the lockdown and has aged two more years since the pandemic. I try not to think about her getting older. She is my and MJ's entire world; she's been with us through it all, so I force my mind not to go there.

Right, where was I? My journey. As a mixed-race woman trying to make it in a predominantly White industry at the time, the ride was not easy but it sure was rewarding. All those years chasing the dream of a Cannes Lion, trying to get into the traditional ad world, landing in digital marketing and then ending up where I am now. I am still beyond grateful. I don't regret a single step that brought me here. The only thing I wish is that I had someone like me to look up to when I was first starting out. But back then, there weren't any women of colour in positions like mine. And that brings me to my next big hustle. I want to become a mentor to young women of colour. I want to be the person I wish I had when I was trying to break into the industry all those years ago.

In a post-apartheid world, there weren't any women of colour working in the creative industry, in positions I wanted, when I was an impressionable young adult. Unlike the medical or science industries, the creative industry had no rule books or manifestos for how to be successful in this field. There was even less guidance out there for women of colour. So I paved my own way, created my own path and made my own rules along the way.

I want this story to be a manifesto for women of colour across the globe. You don't need permission to sit at the table. You have every right to be there, as much as your peers, irrespective of age, race or gender. The norms have changed significantly since I started out on this unexpected career path for a Coloured girl from Wynberg. Thankfully now, it's customary to see women of colour in the creative industry taking up space in leadership positions that used to be filled by White men. Thankfully now, the industry is shifting; there is recognition that the same bland messaging that we keep seeing in the media is not representative of the true population of the world. People of colour bring a different perspective to the ideation table, to the brainstorm. A perspective that's responsible for the diversity you see in the media today. And this is only possible if we are true to ourselves, instead of hiding our identities. Be yourself. Be your most authentic self, because that's when your strengths will truly shine.

I never did get that gold Lion. But if I got what I wanted at the time, which was a job at a creative agency, I would've been on a totally different trajectory in a parallel universe. I would've never been able to move to London and I would've never had the wonderful life I have now. The Butterfly Effect. Maybe we don't always know what's best for us. Maybe sometimes we need to let go of control and just see where the journey takes us. Maybe if we live our lives this way with the faith that everything will work out just fine in the end, we'll end up enjoying the moments more. And ultimately, we'll be living a happier life too because we're not filling those moments of uncertainty with stress and anxiety. Trust in the journey and know that you are exactly where you're meant to be in the end. I know I am.

I pursued London when I was in a place of great pain and heartbreak. I wanted to run away from the place that caused it. I wanted to space and freedom to feel and process the grief of losing my dad. Because I couldn't do that safely in Cape Town, for all of the reasons I've written between the lines in the previous chapters. Maybe in some twisted way, my dad dying was probably the best gift he could've given me. Because if he was still alive, I wouldn't have felt so strongly about wanting to get away from everything that reminded me of him. I wouldn't have made the effort to make London a reality. MJ and I would still be in Cape Town, probably living very different lives to the ones we live now. Thanks God, it all turned out this way. Every cloud has a silver lining, if you're willing and open to seeing it. You know what they say; life can only be lived forwards, and can only be understood backwards.

"I need to write a book," I tell MJ.

He looked at me, one eyebrow lifted, "What kind of book?"

"A book about my experiences, about being a mixed-race female and making it in a predominantly White male industry," I say confidently, like I've never been more sure of anything before in my entire life. MJ's one eyebrow is still lifted as he looks at me quizzically.

"What? You don't think I can write a book? I am a writer, you know."

"I know you can write a book. But will you? Or will this also be something you'll start and won't finish?"

Yes, I've had many ideas in the past that I've started but haven't finished, like the cruelty-free beauty box to raise awareness around animal cruelty, like the alternative clothing line I started in Cape Town, the list goes on. What can I say, I'm an ideas person. I know this about myself. But this is one idea I have to see through. I have the time, and Lord knows I have the words.

"I will write this book. I need to write it,"

For girls like me, I think.

To new beginnings

"For a star to be born, there is one thing that must happen: a gaseous nebula must collapse. So collapse. Crumble. This is not your destruction. This is your birth." — Zoe Skylar

As I walk through the streets of central London after yet another interview for another contract gig, passing red telephone booth after red telephone booth, the sound of a busker performing on the corner catches my attention. He's singing a song I recognise, about driving down winding country lanes, memories of someone special, and sunsets that feel almost unreal. The melody and words hit me in a way I can't shake, stirring a mix of nostalgia and longing that lingers long after the song ends. The mood in the air, the people passing without making eye contact, the world moving and me standing dead still, with this soundtrack in the background, make me feel like the main character in a movie. I think about all the bittersweet memories that make up the broken parts of me. I can't help but wonder what life would be like if my dad was still alive. I'm standing in an ordinary street, living my ordinary life away from the city I grew up in. Away from all the places where I could imagine seeing my dad.

I try to picture him in London with me, with my mum. Would they have visited me together? I wonder. He was a loner just like me, so he probably would've enjoyed moving around on the Underground by himself. He would've thoroughly enjoyed being so close to British football. And with the resources I have access to now, I would've been able to get him a VIP football experience to see his favourite team play. I know he would've loved Sutro. A death in the family is not a once-off event. The loss doesn't end on the day that they die. It's never ending. It's knowing that there's a voice you'll never hear again. A smile you'll never get to see again. A hug you'll never feel again. It's knowing that there's someone in your life that you'll never ever see again. Not in person. Not on a video call. Not even in a photo together of your life right now. The loss is forever and you just learn to live with it. But a little bit of you is lost too, buried there with their flesh and bones underneath the ground. The ground that I never wanted to visit. Not even once. Not even for a little bit. Because the pain almost always felt too real.

I wonder what my dad would think of me now. And I think about where I am, the security I have now, the privileges and opportunities I'm afforded, the new places I get to explore, being able to make my mum's travel dream come true, and all the luxuries that come with being an immigrant in London. I'm definitely not eating white bread and American cheese slices any more from the corner shop in Hammersmith - unless it's from a trendy pop-up in Covent Garden. I'm grateful beyond words.

I think back to 13 years ago, when we stood there in the hallway of the filthy public hospital. Why did they not have any detail about his pre-existing health conditions? Why didn't they at least know that he had a stroke just a few months before? Maybe if we went to a private hospital, maybe they would've been better at checking his pre-existing conditions. Maybe they wouldn't have administered the medicine that sent him into a cardiac arrest. Maybe he'd still be here today. And I say softly to myself, "dear daddy, I wish I had the resources I have now, 13 years ago, so I could go back and save you."

This world has not been kind to him. I make peace with the idea that he is in a better place now, watching down on me. I make peace with his death, and not having enough time to get to know him. A part of me feels a little guilty for feeling that. But I know this is what healing feels like.

As I walked down the escalator at King's Cross St Pancras Underground Station, I glanced up at my reflection in the bright digital billboards that lined the walls flanking the escalator. I see a woman in a faux leather jacket (because we care about animal cruelty now), carrying a large beige puffed laptop bag, long dark hair with faded pink ends tucked into her collar. I don't recognise myself. I look so different to the naive girl that stood on that platform at Heathrow Terminal 5 in April 2015. It feels like an era ago. And I feel like I have lived so much in between the years from then till now. The new person I've become is written all over my face. I came to London battered and bruised and this city took me in and helped me get back up again. And all I can think of is how lucky I am to have a husband who was willing to follow me halfway across the globe so I could follow my dreams and become whole again. I wallow in nostalgia throughout the tube ride home.

The tube stops at Colliers Wood station. I log onto the Underground WiFi and open up my email as my phone connects automatically. 21 698 unread emails in my inbox, but I only open the very first one, the one I've been waiting for, practically my entire career. My heart stops for a minute. I read and re-read that first line of the email over at least twenty times to reassure myself that I'm not dreaming. Could this be? Could I be worthy? Was this really happening to me? A Coloured girl from Cape Town?

I smile. So this is how it all ends, I thought. Or actually, is this how it all starts?

I ran across the street to where MJ and Sutro were waiting for me on the bench in front of the park. I greeted them both with kisses and showed MJ my phone. He looks at my phone and then looks back at me, smiling.

"To new beginnings," we cheered as we read the email again together.

```
Leilah, congratulations on your job offer from
Facebook.
```

Afterword

Reader, she accepted the job offer, obvi. And every day feels like a dream come true.

It's been 3 years since I wrote this book. We're not living in Colliers Wood any more. We asked an estate agent to find us a place in a new neighbourhood where *we* are the most ghetto couple - for safety and vibes. Colliers Wood *was* that when we first discovered it, before it became gentrified and shady.

Earlier this year MJ battled and survived head and neck cancer, which rocked our small London home to its core. We don't chase happy endings any more, because that's not how life works. It ebbs and flows, and you just have to go with the motions and appreciate everything, take the good with the bad, it is all worth it in the end.

MJ is working in the Fintech industry. He works remotely full time so Sutro always has someone at home with her, on days when I occasionally go into the office. We still spend our weekends taking long walks through the park, that end at coffee shops and sometimes dog-friendly burger spots. We revel in the simple life and everyone knows the red chow chow of South West London. We have a community of people who would drop things for us at a moment's notice if we ever needed help. But like dog people, we all only remember each other's dog's names.

After years and years of visa applications and dossiers of paperwork, we finally got our British Citizenship and the golden ticket passport that gives you access to anywhere in the world. We've only seen a handful of places so far, but the world is on our list. We decided to keep our South African citizenship too, for admin purposes.

I taught myself how to rollerskate after a recent trip to Cape Town, when Aimee convinced me to get a pair of quads. Yes, that Aimee. We're still in touch! It was hard doing something for the first time and being bad at it. I wanted to quit many times but it was MJ who insisted I take my skates to the park every day that first few months, and he would sit on the bench after walking Sutro while I'd practice rolling round on 8 wheels. If he didn't push me to continue, I would not be able to call myself a skater right now.

I waited so long to publish this book because I first explored the traditional publishing route. I queried every major publisher I could think of but my story didn't quite resonate; a microcosm of my life.

"I didn't quite connect with the material enough,"

"..it's not right for my list, so I'm going to pass."

"I do not feel it is something we are able to take on and represent at this time."

"Unfortunately, this is not one for us,"

What happens to all the authors whose manuscripts don't get picked up by a publisher? Do their stories remain untold? Brown voices need to be heard too, our stories need to be told. And if you have a story that's brewing inside of you, I think you should just tell it, just write it, no matter how unstructured or unperfect you may think it is - just go for it.

I wrote this initially as a manifesto for brown girls, but really, this is bigger than that. This is for all the under-represented voices all over the world. For anyone who has ever felt trapped, misunderstood, not heard, undervalued, different. For anyone who was ever told, "you can't" - I hope you always know that you can.

I promised you a manifesto, so here it is. Not rules, but guiding principles I carry close to my heart:

1. **Be open to possibility,** but have a plan.
2. **Be a sponge.** Soak up knowledge wherever you can. Learning is a privilege; if you have access to it, use it to grow in every part of your life.
3. **Remember: your job title does not define you.** Any role can be made rewarding if you bring curiosity and passion to it.
4. **You can always begin again.** At any age, at any stage, as many times as it takes.
5. **Be kind to yourself.** Invest in your own growth, through learning, healing, and building a lifestyle that supports you.

6. **Be unapologetically yourself.** Life flows easier when you stop people-pleasing and start honouring your own values. Stand for what you believe in.
7. **If it doesn't open, it's not your door.** Let go of what isn't meant for you. The less you cling, the easier it is to move forward.
8. **Find a workplace that fits your spirit.** I know that's a privilege, but trust me, the alignment is worth everything.
9. **When you've made it to the top, it's your job to send the elevator back down.**

And finally:

- **[Enter yours here.]** Because every manifesto is unfinished. It grows with you.

Acknowledgements

The names of the digital marketing agencies in this book have been changed for obvious reasons. The stories themselves, however, are true to my lived experience. Similarly, the details about my visa process should not be taken as an official guide or legal advice; it is simply the record of my own journey. Now that the legalities are out of the way..

The biggest thank you/shukran to my mum Shienaaz Adams who raised me to be exactly who I am today; I love who I turned out to be and all merit goes to you, mummy.

I couldn't have gotten this far and written this book without the support of the very best husband, life partner and fur baby co-parent, MJ; you are my world.

A thank you must also go to my family, ouma Dia's children, Adeela, Sedicka, Zahier, Ish, Boychies, and the OG Friday night Aneesas crew: Rifaat, Darwees, Ilo, Saara, Daanyaal, Rayhaan, Daiyaan and Yushaa. You've all contributed to my journey in some way, some of you even financially. Thank you for betting on me and for always believing that I was better than I actually am.

To my darling friend Elizabeth Darke, who made me feel at

home in London, who kept me sane during some of the most trying chapters of my career, who listened with patience as I vented endlessly about the smallest details of work. The fact that you're still my friend after all that is proof of your saintliness. I cherish you, Liz.

To all the great managers I crossed paths with along the way, especially Peter Wood, thank you for letting me be me.

To everyone who was kind enough to be my beta testers, who gave me feedback and helped to critique my writing. This book only turned out the way it did because of you.

Thanks to the people who checked in, mentors who nudged me forward, colleagues who taught me what to do (and sometimes what *not* to do), you all shaped this journey in ways big and small. This book is not mine alone; it is a tapestry woven from your care, guidance and belief.

& For my dad who is no longer with us, thank you for the lessons you didn't know you taught me. I wish everyday that you are happy where you are now, and proud of who I've become.

About the Author

Leilah van der Schyff (née Jumat) is a South African-born author and creative professional whose work explores identity, growth, and belonging through the lens of race, gender, and culture. Her debut memoir, *Brown Girl Manifesto*, draws on her lived experience of breaking barriers and amplifying under-represented voices in global industries. With over 18 years of experience in advertising and technology across South Africa and the United Kingdom, Leilah has received numerous accolades for creative excellence. She actively mentors through programs that promote gender and educational equality. When she's not writing and designing, she spends her time with her husband and their dog, exploring and photographing London's most charming dog-friendly spots.

You can connect with me on:
🌐 https://www.instagram.com/browngirlmanifesto

www.ingramcontent.com/pod-product-compliance
Lightning Source LLC
Chambersburg PA
CBHW020358080526
44584CB00014B/1080